A Guide to Sources in Educational Media and Technology

by

Dorothy T. Taggart

The Scarecrow Press, Inc.
Metuchen, N.J.   1975

Library of Congress Cataloging in Publication Data

Taggart, Dorothy T   1917-
    A guide to sources in educational media and technology.

    Includes indexes.
    1. Audio-visual education--Bibliography. 2. Educational technology--Bibliography. I. Title.
Z5814.V8T33   016.37133   74-26849
ISBN 0-8108-0781-5

Copyright 1975 by Dorothy T. Taggart

To my Mother

For her determination, her great courage
And indomitable spirit, as well as for
Her love of life

PREFACE

The field of educational media and technology is a rapidly expanding one of growing interest to students and teachers. There is unprecedented growth in the use of media in teaching and learning and in collections for study or reading in the university and school library media center or learning resources center. This book has been written to aid the librarian in finding the materials that both he and the teaching staff, as well as the student, need. The terms educational technology, educational media, instructional technology, audiovisual instruction and instructional media all point to the role that new tools and teaching materials are playing in education today. Teachers need to understand the potential of newer educational media and to know the great advantages of media use in improving classroom instruction. Librarians need to know and to have available materials in many areas of media instruction. Students are interested in new means of communication and learning.

This bibliography is not intended as a collection for a particular subject-matter field or for any one grade level. However, the author does have in mind a well-balanced and up-to-date collection for the university library in the field of educational media and technology. Many university and college libraries today are seeking the best and newest books in the field; many are lacking in a good collection in educational media. On the secondary and elementary level, the author has in mind a collection for the professional library for teachers, books to turn to as the teacher begins to use many media in the classroom.

The divisions of the book are selected because they are subjects of most interest in teaching with new media today. The book is a guide to books and periodicals, books which have been surveyed and read with use by students and teachers in mind. It is planned that the publication be regularly updated and that it keep pace with the development and use of educational media and technology. The author welcomes suggestions from those teaching and working with students in the field. In design and content, the book reflects the organization and plan of a course in bibliography of educational media originated by the author, who teaches on the university level and is also a librarian of a school library media center with an independent study concept using many newer media.

The hope of the author is that the publication will be a useful book, valuable to graduate students in the field of educational technology, to school librarians and administrators, to the university and college librarian, and to teachers in courses in educational technology. Terminology is based on those terms most commonly used in the field of educational media and technology today; in cases where there are various subject titles in use, the author has relied on the ones used by ERIC, the ERIC Clearinghouse on Educational Media and Technology, Stanford University, Stanford, California. The section on periodicals is limited to acquisition information only, with specific subject coverage noted by the section topics and sub-topics.

Dorothy Taggart

TABLE OF CONTENTS

	Preface	v
	Contents	vii
1.	History of the Audiovisual Movement	1
2.	Selection of Media Materials	7
3.	Facility Planning	16
4.	Instructional Film and Television	21
5.	Programed Instruction	33
6.	Computer Assisted Instruction	40
7.	Design and Production of Instructional Materials	50
8.	Pre-Service and In-Service Training of Teachers	56
9.	Administration of Educational Media	63
10.	Media in Curriculum Design	68
11.	Instructional Systems Analysis, Design and Development	74
12.	System Evaluation	84
13.	Learning Theory	89
14.	Media Research	96
15.	Aspects of Change	106

16.	Select Bibliography of Periodicals on Educational Media	113
17.	Professional Organizations	130
18.	Indexes	134
19.	Addresses of Publishers	137
	Index of Authors	145
	Index of Titles	150

Chapter 1

HISTORY OF THE AUDIOVISUAL MOVEMENT

"Education has come a long way in the last fifty years from using audiovisuals as casual enrichment 'aids' to a wide acceptance of the concept of instructional technology as an intellectual process of instructional planning" writes Jerrold E. Kemp in the fiftieth anniversary edition of <u>Audiovisual Instruction,</u> the official publication of the Association for Educational Communications and Technology, published in March 1973. Technology has swept through our world bringing many changes in manufacturing, communications, the space age, the military and education. New media are no longer "new" media to many teachers teaching in our schools today; education is keeping pace with industry in many schools of our nation. But a history of the audiovisual movement is of interest to many in education--a stop along the way to realize how far we have gone and where the future lies.

Visual education was the term first used for classroom use of the earliest technological materials. St. Louis, in 1905, was the first school system to start a visual education department, making weekly deliveries of instructional materials to its schools. Others soon followed, with smaller school systems depending on film-lending libraries of a few large universities. The schools in the Midwest led the way with four such units opened in 1914, at the Universities of Kansas, Iowa, Iowa State and Wisconsin.

Research in the visual education field in the early 1920's was important. A NEA committee was appointed in 1923 to study the value of motion pictures in education. In 1928 Ben D. Wood, Columbia University, and Frank N. Freeman, University of Chicago, published an extensive study of the use of films in twelve major U.S. cities. The 1923-1945 period was one of great conflict: should the concentration be on 16mm. film or another size, silent or sound, or on other media? The 35mm. filmstrip projector came on the market in 1925; first used chiefly in industrial training, it became one of the most widely used types of projection for still pictures, and is widely used even today.

Advancing technology changed the term <u>visual education</u> to <u>audiovisual education</u>. Today teachers teaching in the best schools of our nation have at their fingertips the resources of special school-building collections housed in school library media centers or in system-wide centers--materials for teaching, not just supplementary to teaching. Such centers are variously called visual education department, audiovisual center, learning resources center, instructional materials center, curriculum materials center, instructional technology center, audiovisual communication center, communications center and media center.

Today's educational goals must rely on the development of technological services, although this realization has come slowly to education. It is true that the successful use of educational media must depend upon good teaching in the classroom by well-trained and good teachers, and upon integrated use of many kinds of teaching materials. Today's teacher-education institutions and today's schools must prepare for the future by building a backlog of staff experience in using technological media and methods to make teaching effective. Development of instructional programs demands staff and leaders, effective organization and cooperation and adequate financial support.

"The newer educational media will be accepted or rejected," writes Kenneth D. Norberg, "as means to ends. People who try new tools do so to accomplish new tasks or to perform old tasks in a new and better way. These are not just strong and ingenious tools; they are also means that will be used to accomplish some purpose beyond their own use, to implement some program. They challenge educators to take another look at their goals, both explicit and implicit, to determine whether the goals are still sound, to decide whether the new media will help to implement them, possibly to change the course of the instructional program as well as the lives of the teachers and students who are involved."

1. Barnouw, Erik. A History of Broadcasting in the United States. 3 vols. Oxford University Press, 1966-70.
 A well-written, comprehensive and excellent history of broadcasting. This book is an interesting history of broadcasting, with thorough discussion, analysis, documentation and illustration.

2. Carlson, Richard O. Adoption of Educational Innovations. The Center for the Advanced Study of Educational Administration, University of Oregon, 1965.
 A basic historical survey which discusses the rate of adoption of educational innovations. This is a valuable background study for the school system considering educational innovations--a critical study.

3. Godfrey, Eleanor P. The State of Educational Technology: 1961-1966. Monograph 3, Department of Audiovisual Instruction, NEA, 1967.

A critical examination of what school districts have made of audiovisual technology over a critical six-year period. Resources, use of resources, prospects for the future are discussed. It is basically an excellent proposal for further research study.

4. Lamb, Robert Thomas Bryden. <u>Aids to Modern Teaching: a Short Survey.</u> Isaac Pitman, 1967.

As we move toward a multi-media or systems approach to education, courses must be planned to use the optimum media at every stage. System analysis of programmed learning may be applied to all teaching media. The book discusses major teaching aids, including many media.

5. Martin, W.T. <u>Curriculum Improvement and Innovation: A Partnership of Students, School Teachers and Research Scholars,</u> edited by W.T. Martin and Dan C. Pinck, with an introduction by Howard W. Johnson. Robert Bentley, 1966.

The book details the development and history of Educational Services Incorporated (ESI) which began at Massachusetts Institute of Technology, a partnership of teachers, scholars and students which after two years of intensive work resulted in the PSCS physics course. ESI now has responsibilities for nine school curriculum projects, with 450 faculty members from 228 colleges and universities and 400 school teachers working full or parttime on ESI's programs in curriculum development and teacher education. The book is a history of the diversity and profound effect on education which has resulted from the work of teachers, scholars and students together in ESI.

6. McBeath, Ronald J. <u>Extending Education Through Technology: Selected Writings by James D. Finn on Instructional Technology,</u> edited by Ronald J. McBeath. AECT, 1972.

The editor brings together the writings of James D. Finn, dividing them into four sections: Criticisms, Traditions and Challenges; Automation and Education; From Audiovisual to Instructional Technology; Commitment to the Future. His leadership in instructional technology spans more than 25 years.

7. Pula, Fred John. <u>Technology in Education: Challenge and Change,</u> by Fred John Pula and Robert J. Goff. Charles A. Jones Publishing Company, 1972.

A collection of articles published in the last twenty

History of the Audiovisual Movement 5

years; as a survey of the field and its problems this book is of value. It is well-organized in three basic divisions: Foundations of Education and Educational Technology, Tools of Instruction, and Educational Technology and Organization for Educational Technology.

8. Saettler, Paul. A History of Instructional Technology. McGraw-Hill, 1968.
    A good background for a systems approach to instruction. A first history of instructional technology, bringing together and into focus the theoretical and methodological foundations of audio-visual materials and instructional technology. Written with the encouragement of James D. Finn, an outstanding leader in the field of instructional technology. Chapters include an introductory one on the meaning of instructional technology, pre-1700 forerunners of instructional technology, the period 1700-1900, and the time to the present.
    This detailed history covers many areas of use of educational media, including film, the audiovisual movement itself, industry and military use of instructional technology, instructional radio, television and programed instruction. The final section, a background of instructional media research, is a conclusive and important contribution of the book. The concluding chapter is a forward-looking one, discussing problems and prospects of instructional technology.

9. Trow, William Clark. Teacher and Technology: New Design for Learning. Appleton-Century-Crofts, 1963.
    The historical development of instructional media is reviewed, with emphasis on new concepts and new demands of new technology. Television, programed learning and systems organization in the school are discussed. Directions of change emphasize rate of change. New media must be integrated into all of education, with accompanying readjustments in organization and procedure.

10. Trump, J. Lloyd. Focus on Change: Guide to Better Schools, by J. Lloyd Trump and Dorsey Baynham. Rand-McNally, 1961.
    Complexity of the problem demands unprecedented, many-sided solutions. Changing schedules, staffing, reorganization of instruction, and uses of new technological media--all are discussed. One of the early thought-provoking books for the educator, important to the history of the audiovisual movement.

11. Unwin, Derick. Aspects of Educational Technology, by

Derick Unwin and John Leedham. The proceedings of the Programmed Learning Conference held at Loughborough, April 15-18, 1966. Methuen, 1967.

Discusses programmed learning in schools, in industry and in higher education. Contains 43 papers detailing the state of technology in 1966, both in England and in the United States.

Chapter 2

SELECTION OF MEDIA MATERIALS

Meeting the instructional needs of the learner requires excellent instructional materials, excellent teachers, cooperative parents and rich, challenging experiences both in and out of school, says Edgar Dale, writing in <u>Audiovisual Instruction</u>, "Toward Excellence in Instruction," September 1973.

We are considering improved instructional experiences in all fields of learning today, both in the classroom and out. Changes in the needs and interests of students, in modern life, and in the curriculum demand many resources for learning.

Selection of those materials is the responsibility of many of us today in our nation's schools and universities and colleges. Leslie Cottardi, writing on "A Survey of Instructional Budgets" in <u>Audiovisual Instruction</u>, December 1971, points out that money for instructional materials in our schools is only an average of five percent of the nationally recommended amount. Most school districts, however, are increasing expenditures. Teachers, administrators and librarians are all involved in selection of instructional materials.

In a survey done by Myles P. Breen and Donald A. Ary ("A Nationwide Survey to Determine Who Chooses Instructional Films"), of some 174 school districts selected from the 14,000 listed in Education Almanac (1970), the individual teacher was cited as the most important element in film selection by 54.5 percent of the respondents; teacher committees were cited by 28.7 percent of the respondents. Administrators also have an important voice in film selection; 45.5 percent of the respondents in the Breen and Ary study indicated that building principals are involved in selection. And 40.5 percent of the respondents named the librarian as the person who makes or shares in the selection decision. Such selection involvements often carry over into the selection of all media, with the possible exception of books, in the library media center.

Considerable financial support for audiovisual equipment and materials has come from the federal aid to education programs. The National Defense Education Act of 1958 provided funds that enabled local school units to purchase audiovisual equipment and materials for the purpose of strengthening instructional programs in selected curriculum areas. The Elementary and Secondary Education Act of 1965 was the largest single commitment by the federal government to strengthen and improve the educational quality of schools. Title II recognized that teaching and learning depend upon effective school library materials, high quality up-to-date textbooks and a variety of other educational resources. Such federal support increased in dollar support in the 1970 fiscal school year, but the percentage of the total expenditure decreased one percent in comparison to the two previous fiscal school years.

The teacher of today realizes that motivation to learn is the key to excellence in instruction. The roles of teacher and student are changing as we aim toward individualization of instruction. Every classroom can have the best in instructional materials now produced. Excellence in learning involves use of many educational media as the student learns to read critically, listen critically and observe critically. As the librarian, teacher or administrator selects media materials for the learning resource center, the library media center or the classroom, he must evaluate effectiveness of resources in meeting objectives (design), production standards, acceptability for acquisition, and whether the resources meet a specific need (utilization). Evaluation must precede selection. The supply-support function includes evaluation, selection, acquisition, distribution/retrieval, description and storage functions.

Basic indexes and catalogs are used by every librarian selecting material and recommending selection aids to the teacher or administrator. This list of selection sources is intended to bring up-to-date selection in certain areas, to point out some sources which discuss selection criteria, and to list important selection sources for the teacher, administrator and librarian.

12. Allison, Mary L. New Educational Materials, Pre-Kindergarten Through Grade 12. Citation Press, 1967.
A compilation of evaluations by teachers, librarians and curriculum specialists of materials for all subjects. A final section lists sources for all materials listed. A good beginning source for pre-service and in-service training of teachers; a practical listing.

13. Anderson, Robert M. Instructional Resources for Teachers of the Culturally Disadvantaged and Exceptional; compiled and edited by Robert M. Anderson, Robert E. Hemenway and Janet W. Anderson. Charles C. Thomas, 1969.
A fine and comprehensive listing of instructional resources for teachers and administrators. The authors have attempted systematically to identify instructional materials

which they consider to be effective teaching materials and resources. This book does not include materials for the gifted student. There is an intended emphasis on remedial and adapted instructional material. At the preschool and elementary levels, selections emphasize experimental and stimulation instructional materials and aids. Chapters are concerned with particular areas of study--social sciences, mathematics, reading and English, etc.

14. Audiovisual Resources for Teaching Instructional Technology: An Annotated Listing. 3d ed. Area of Instructional Technology, Syracuse University, 1971.

A comprehensive listing of audiovisual materials related to the activities of instructional materials coordinators, consultants, instructors in instructional technology programs, audiovisual specialists, librarians and students. Includes all areas: administration, facilities, instructional design, learning and communications, media equipment, media production, media utilization, research, instructional techniques. Descriptive annotations.

15. Beilby, Albert. Audiovisual Resources for Teaching. Syracuse University, 1971.

A comprehensive listing of film, cartridge, record, filmstrip, slide, tape, videotape and transparency titles, along with sources for use in instructional technology. Brief annotations. Materials are categorized for their relevance to administration, facilities, instructional design, etc.

16. Blue Book of Audiovisual Materials. 47th ed. Educational Screen and Audiovisual Guide, 1972.

This yearly publication includes all materials in 33 subject fields at all grade levels. Includes approximately 200 titles produced in the 12 months preceding publication. Has title index.

17. Brown, James W. AV Instruction: Media and Methods. McGraw-Hill, 1969.

A fine book written to help prospective and practicing teachers become properly acquainted with the broad range and interrelated uses of many different kinds of educational media, techniques and devices. The most valuable part of the book for those involved in the selection of materials is the section at the end of each chapter on particular subjects. There is a valuable Subject Field Reference Guide listing materials and their uses.

Selection of Media Materials   11

18. Charnes, A. and others. LP II--A Goal Programming Model for Media. Northwestern University, 1967.
   Valuable for the concept of a goal-programming model for selecting media. Alters the objective and extends previous media models by accounting for cumulative duplicating audiences over a variety of time periods.

19. Chisholm, Margaret E. Media Indexes and Review Sources. School of Library and Information Services, University of Maryland, 1972.
   A listing of publications containing evaluative reviews, prepared as a buying guide and as a means of locating nonprint materials. A discussion of the major indexes is valuable.

20. Educational Media Index: A Project of the Educational Media Council. McGraw-Hill, 1964-
   Includes approximately 28,000 titles of all types of educational materials, from kindergarten through college level and adult education. Use of symbols before descriptive entries denotes type of medium and key to 14 symbols which appears in lower left-hand corner of each even-numbered page. Master title index.

21. Educators Progress Service, Inc. Guide to Free Films. Guide to Free Filmstrips. Educator's Guide to Free Tapes, Scripts and Transcripts. Educator's Guide to Free Guidance Materials. Educators Progress Service, all yearly.
   These catalogs list many free materials and are a useful addition to the professional library for selection of media materials.

22. Entelek CAI/CMI/PI Information Exchange. Entelek, Inc., 1965 to date.
   Currently released computer-assisted (CAI) computer-managed (CMI) and programmed instruction (PI) programs in all subject fields and grade levels. Also includes index cards for currently released CAI, CMI and PI research reports and descriptions of CAI facilities. Numerical arrangement according to Entelek serial number is used.

23. Erickson, Carlton W. H. Administering Instructional Media Programs. Macmillan, 1968.
   A broad and comprehensive book which deals primarily with technological media, discussing the complexity that has developed in the field. There is a quite complete

listing of materials on each subject at the end of each chapter. It is valuable in selection of media materials because of its breadth, selectivity and inclusiveness.

24. Erickson, Carlton, W. H. Fundamentals of Teaching with Audiovisual Technology. Macmillan, 1965.
Although written for the undergraduate student preparing for a career in teaching, the book will facilitate the kind of thinking by teachers which will relate audiovisual technology meaningfully to teaching in the classroom. All chapters include available technological materials for class use; good recommendations for teacher or librarian.

25. Films and Filmstrips on Audio-Visual Materials and Methods. Rev. ed. Educational Film Library Association, Inc., 1971.
An exclusive list on all phases of the audiovisual field, this book also has an excellent directory of sources. Intended for teachers, audiovisual coordinators or directors, and for students in AV education courses.

26. Freedman, Florence B. The Classroom Teacher's Guide to Audio-Visual Materials, by Florence B. Freedman and Esther L. Berg. Chilton, 1966.
A brief but complete description of many audiovisual aids, bringing up-to-date the 1961 edition. Instructional materials and educational media are described and emphasis is upon use, related to specific teaching fields. Principally, its approach is for the elementary or junior high teacher. The section, A Guide to Resources, is a brief bibliography which contains general references, periodicals, a general source list and sources of free and inexpensive materials. The list of producers and distributors is brief and not complete enough for present-day use.

27. Gaver, Mary V. The Elementary School Library Collection. 6th ed. Newark, Bro-Dart Foundation, 1971.
A source book for elementary librarians for selection of materials. Includes a basic beginning collection and "opening day" collection; Phases II and III bring the collection to 8000 books and 200 audiovisual items. The book is based on the work of an advisory committee and a selection committee. They have assembled an excellent, well organized collection.

28. Great Plains National Instructional Television Library. 1972 Recorded Instruction for Television: Elementary,

Selection of Media Materials

Secondary, Adult, College and In-Service. University of Nebraska, 1972.

A listing of all materials currently offered by Great Plains National Instructional Television Library, arranged according to subject-matter, giving full description of materials. The catalog also details the services available from GPNITL. A well-organized listing of available television materials.

29. Jones, Milbrey L. Sources of Audiovisual Materials. U. S. Government Printing Office, 1967.

The program specialist, School Libraries Section, Department of Health, Education and Welfare, Office of Education, has prepared this bibliography of books and other materials available in educational media. It contains a directory of publishers.

30. Lanier, Vincent. The Use of Newer Media in Art Education Project. National Art Association, 1966.

The impact of educational technology on art instruction was studied during a five-day symposium by 50 art educators and four media specialists. The publication is valuable for uses of media discussed.

31. Mountain Plains Educational Media Council. Film Catalog, 1973-1975. Mountain Plains EMC, 1973.

This selection catalog is included here as a fine collection and example of selection aids being prepared by many schools across the country. It is well-indexed with subject-heading index and alphabetical title listing.

32. Multi-Media Reviews Index. Pierian Press, annual.

The 1972 MMRI indexes some 214 publications, with approximately 30,000 citations and cross references. This is supplemented monthly in Audiovisual Instruction and by separately published tri-quarterly supplements beginning in 1973. This updating service was begun in the October 1971 issue of Audiovisual Instruction.

33. Plunkett, Dalton. Stimulus Ideas for Using Selected Educational Media. Northwest Library Service, Inc., 1970.

Designed to stimulate creative use of the motion picture projector, 8 mm. loop projector, slide and filmstrip projector, overhead projector, opaque projector and tape recorder. Although simply written and very brief, it is a book of excellent ideas.

34. Rowell, John. Educational Media Selection Centers: Identification and Analysis of Current Practices, by John Rowell and M. Ann Heidbreder. American Library Association, 1971.
A research study funded by the National Book Committee, the U.S. Office of Education, and the Center for Documentation and Communication Research of Case Western University. The purpose was to contribute to the development of quality education by improving the selection and use of educational media. Facilities and programs which introduce teachers, librarians and other concerned professional adults to a wide range of media that exist at the state, regional and local levels to support and supplement education were examined, and successful components evaluated.

35. Rufsvold, Margaret I. and Carolyn Guss. Guides to Newer Educational Media: Films, Filmstrips, Kinescopte, Phonodiscs, Phonotapes, Programmed Instruction Materials, Slides, Transparencies, Videotapes. 2nd ed. American Library Association, 1967.

36. Rufsvold, Margaret I. and Carolyn Guss. Guides to Educational Media, 3rd edition. American Library Association, 1971.
An updated guide to catalogs and lists, services of professional organizations, and certain specialized periodicals which systematically provide information on the newer educational media. Descriptive annotations for each detail their scope, arrangement, entries and special features. An added section to the earlier edition is a listing of media catalogs and lists published since 1957 but unavailable in 1971. It is indexed by author, publisher, title, subject and type of material.

37. University of Colorado. 1971 National Center for Audio Tapes Supplement. University of Colorado, 1971.
Updates but does not entirely supersede an earlier publication, 1970-72 National Center for Audio Tapes Catalog. Listing some 12,000 tapes, the catalog provides an expanding and continually growing source of instructional material. The recordings are selected on the basis of curricular relevance and production quality. The catalog is well-organized and contains a subject index, descriptive listings as well as alphabetically listed producer codes.

38. University of Colorado. Guidelines for Audio Tape Libraries. University of Colorado, n.d.

Selection of Media Materials					15

Since an audio tape library is a part of even the smaller school media center today, this handbook on organization and care of the audio library is of value to the librarian or media specialist who is selecting and organizing tapes.

39. United States Atomic Energy Commission. __Combined Film Catalog__, 1972.
The 1972 revision of the __USAEC Combined Film Catalog__ describes 232 films in two major film collections: Education--Information and Technical-Professional. All domestic film libraries have been consolidated into one new library. An excellent source for films.

40. Westinghouse Learning Corporation. __1972-1973 Learning Directory Supplement__. Westinghouse Learning Corporation, 1972.
An up-to-date index of instructional materials in all media, the directory has 75,000 entries under more than 28,000 topics, representing 24,000 items published in 1971 and 1972. The basic __1970-71 Learning Directory__ lists all available educational materials published prior to 1971. This supplement may be used independently of the earlier volume.

41. Winan, Raymond V. __Instructional Materials__. Charles A. Jones, 1972.
A ready-reference book for the teacher which covers many media. The bibliography at the end of the book lists sources of materials vital to additional training in uses of all materials discussed. In his preface, Winan states that "although a wide range of commercially produced material is available, instructional materials prepared by teachers frequently offer the most practical approach to specific learning situations."

42. Wittich, Walter Arno and Charles Francis Schuller. __Instructional Technology: Its Nature and Use__. 5th edition. Harper & Row, 1972.
This up-to-date revision of a standard book emphasizes ways and means of helping people to learn by using creatively a wide range of materials and equipment that involve looking and listening. Bibliographies are excellent selection aids for the classroom teacher or librarian.

Chapter 3

FACILITY PLANNING

One of the best publications on facility planning is not included in this bibliography because of its early copyright date (1963) and because it is discussed at length in this introduction. The School Library by Ralph E. Ellsworth and Hobart D. Wagener, published by Educational Facilities Laboratories, is one of the most detailed and comprehensive publications on the subject of facility planning. It is a forward-looking book, as applicable today as when it was published in 1963; it is well-illustrated and should be in the collection of sources for any librarian or school planning new facilities. Much that is written is adaptable to all levels of education, college to elementary.

"Many of the innovations in our secondary schools are of collegiate nature," write the authors of The School Library. Independent study, honors programs, the progress of a student according to his individual interests, free time scheduling--all are characteristics of today's schools in many areas, particularly on the college level. The basis of new planning of facilities is this reorganization of the schedule of classes to meet student needs and interests. Students must have access to many sources of knowledge; all do not seek knowledge in the same way and the physical environment has much to do with learning.

In the modern library the student is comfortable, relaxed and free to seek his own sources, whether book or nonbook. We try many means to motivate students to learn--to read and to listen. The ideas of self-teaching are not new. They are the basis of the Oxford and Cambridge libraries and concept of education, and of institutions like Princeton University in this country. The trend of our secondary schools, as well as our elementary schools, is following that set by higher education: to provide materials for the student to learn, give him a setting where he will have full use of such materials and freedom to use them as he wishes.

Up until about 1960 good teaching was considered the vehicle for good learning; all depended on the teacher. An official statement issued by the American Association of School Librarians in 1956 stressed the concept of the central school library as a place where all kinds of learning materials are found. The executive board of the American Association of School Librarians and the Association of College and Research Libraries, both divisions of the American Library Association, and the Department of Audiovisual Instruction of the National Education Association approved a statement in 1958 emphasizing the same approach to library resource materials. Finally, in 1960, the <u>Standards for School Library Programs</u> were produced by the American Association of School Librarians in cooperation with nineteen other groups, recognizing the incorporation of all learning materials in the library. In 1966 a revision of the AASL <u>Standards</u> was published, revising and bringing up-to-date the 1960 <u>Standards</u>.

Many names are used for the center of the school's

program of learning: educational media center, school media center, library media center, educational resource center, learning resource center, and variations of all of these terms.

The field of educational technology is the focus for the new concept of learning in the school. The center of this focus is the library, although in many schools this concept faces opposition. Central to an integrated approach to learning, however, is the necessity to utilize all available resources. Many must be involved in planning and in utilization of learning resources. Innovative learning environments must be adapted to the needs of the school and may or may not be centered in the learning resource center itself. Such instructionally developed approaches to education should be planned for, however, in the development of a learning center.

The field of educational technology and its program in the school must concern itself with the learner, with individualization, and with making learning more personal. There should be development of a wide range of resources and use of the systems approach to the facilitation of learning. This is where facility planning in all its specifics is important. We must be concerned with what we do with materials in order to achieve our purpose--maximum learning. Resources, activities, development of resources, production and location of instructional materials, organization and utilization--all are the concern of the library and its staff. The design and planning of the center is basic to the whole concept of educational technology and its use in the schools. This bibliography offers new concepts and ideas for planning the modern school media center, the learning resource center of the school.

Facility Planning

43. Barson, John and Gardner M. Jones. A Procedural and Cost Analysis Study of Media in Instructional Systems Development, Part A and B. Michigan State University, 1965.
   A two-part study which identifies the factors which contribute to successful media innovation and instructional development and establishes guidelines to serve others. A proposal for institutions of higher education is included.

44. Educational Facilities Laboratories. The Greening of the High School, by Ruth Weinstock. EFL, 1973.
   A report of the EFL/IDEA symposium of August, 1972 on how to make high schools more effective facilities for helping their students. Architects, superintendents, principals, teachers, and school planners attended.

45. Educational Facilities Laboratories. New Buildings on Campus: Six Designs for a College Communications Center. Educational Facilities Laboratories, 1963.
   Not a recent publication but a far-seeing one with ideas for today's designer of learning resource centers on the college and university campus.

46. Green, Alan C., ed. Educational Facilities with New Media, by Alan C. Green, editor, with M. C. Gassman, Wayne F. Koppes, Raymond D. Caravaty and Davis S. Haviland. Department of Audiovisual Instruction (now Association for Educational Communications and Technology), NEA, with Center for Architectural Research, Rensselaer Polytechnic Institute, 1966.
   The final report of an architectural research study conducted by the staff of the Center for Architectural Research, School of Architecture, Rensselaer Polytechnic Institute, New York. The objective of the publication is to optimize the conditions for learning by providing physical environments most conducive to learning when media are employed in the educational process. Data, design studies, planning premises, reactions and conclusions have been collected and organized to offer guidance in the programming and planning of appropriate educational facilities.

47. Hertzberg, Alvin. Schools Are for Children: An Approach to the Open Classroom. Schocken Books, 1971.
   An excellent resource book for educators or boards planning open classroom programs. It presents detailed physical layouts and programs to be used in the open classroom, all recommended and discussed. Illustrated.

48. Iowa State Department of Public Instruction. Plan for Progress in the Media Center. Iowa State Department of Public Instruction, 1969. (Available from DPS, Publications Division, Grimes State Office Building, Des Moines, Iowa.)

49. New Spaces for Learning. Center for Architectural Research, School of Architecture, Rensselaer Polytechnic Institute, Troy, New York, 1966.
    This revision of the 1961 publication provides guidance for the design and planning of media-oriented learning spaces focused on the student user of both small and large-group rooms. Design studies are included as well as documentation of a case study demonstration.

50. Pearson, Neville P. Instructional Materials Centers: Selected Readings, by Neville P. Pearson and Lucius Butler. Burgess Publishing Company, 1969.
    An excellent collection of readings describing and advocating the design of instructional materials centers to meet needs of today's schools.

51. Standards for School Media Programs, 1969. American Library Association or National Education Association, 1969.
    Prepared by a joint committee of the American Association of School Librarians (ALA) and the Department of Audiovisual Instruction of the National Education Association in cooperation with representatives from twenty-eight professional and civic organizations. Brings standards for school library media centers in line with needs and requirements of today's educational goals and coordinates standards for school library and audiovisual programs. The Standards describe the services of the media program in the school and note the necessary requirements for staff, resources and facilities to implement the program effectively.

Chapter 4

INSTRUCTIONAL FILM AND TELEVISION

Television is one of the great electronic devices McLuhan sees as prime shapers of our changing world. This powerful medium can teach with great effectiveness. In a report entitled <u>Learning by Television</u>, Murphy and Gross conclude that "Television <u>works</u> as an educational tool. There is no question of its validity as a medium of instruction. Students can learn from television, as they can from teachers and texts, radio, recordings and film. But educators are still far from grasping the real nature and potential of television."

Speaking of the ability of electronic media to support education, William G. Harley of the National Association of Broadcasters told a Senate committee, "Educational television and radio provide unique methods for organizing for innovation and change. Properly integrated into the school system, they can help improve the quality of instruction, enrich the curriculum and extend the benefits of such schooling to millions of children who will otherwise be deprived of opportunities that should be open to them."

It is important that we employ new tools and new methods if we are to adequately equip our children to live in tomorrow's world. There are many tools of communication which are available for educational use. In its report on

Automation and Technology in Education, the Joint Economic Committee of the Congress of the United States says, "The technological aids which were brought to the committee's attention include educational television, both open and closed (circuit); video tape, computerized instruction; the use of computers for student testing, guidance and evaluation, and the storage, retrieval and distribution of information; programmed courses for instruction; teaching machines, particularly the 'talking typewriter,' the use of microfilm and microfilm viewing equipment; and language laboratories."

The newer media of education, and particularly educational television and film, may be used to help individualize instruction for a larger number of students, with superior results. Concerning the importance of individualized instruction, B. F. Skinner, "father" of programmed instruction, says, "It is important that the student should learn without being taught, solve problems by himself, explore the unknown, and behave in unusual ways, and these _activities_ should, if possible, be taught.... To teach a student to study is to teach him techniques of self-management which will increase the likelihood that what is seen or heard will be remembered." The role of the teacher is changing. He must become the guide to the means and sources of education, a selector of experiences and processes for the students, and a personal counselor. His role must no longer be that of the one and only source of all knowledge and experience. We are going to have to treat each one of the millions of children as the individual he is. The labor-saving techniques of electronic teaching, of systematic instruction, and of electronic information processing devices, are the means by which we will be able to win the time and capabilities to accomplish this goal.

In a discussion of instructional television in higher education, the focus of attention is on instructional uses of various forms rather than on their utilization in general administration, student personnel programs or research. Educators first thought of using television primarily as a means of increasing efficiency by multiplying the professor's audience, but it became apparent that this was an undesirable use of the medium. The present pressing problem is to develop courses and materials that are worth televising, rather than to plan new and more complicated physical installations.

A self-contained classroom television system--camera, videotape recorder and monitor--offers exciting possibilities for all sorts of teaching, including the development of true team-teaching approaches, combining the talents of many teachers. Many interesting case studies are found in New Media and College Teaching, by James W. Thornton, Jr. and James Brown.

The most thorough of the survey studies, A National Survey and Current Utilization of In-School Closed-Circuit Television and Instructional Television Fixed Services, completed and published in 1967 by the Department of Audiovisual Instruction, National Education Association, had as its ultimate goal to encourage the use of CCTV and ITFS as tools which can play an important part in improving the quality of instruction. Similar annual surveys from 1957 through 1960, the research reported by the Technological Development Project of the National Education Association in a publication popularly known as Occasional Paper No. 10--all were concerned with the growth and development of television in education. The most important contribution of such research and studies is that they facilitate communication among institutions operating or planning instructional television systems. They provide a benchmark against which to measure the impact of existing and future efforts.

There are many important questions yet to be answered in the field of instructional television. Are standards being developed? What direction should current research take? How will instructional television programming be distributed in the years ahead? How much are teachers of the future learning about the uses and values of educational technology in our teacher-education institutions?

Every educational innovation requires a recognized and identifiable educational need, a means for satisfying this need, and an educational institution willing and able to engage in the experiment. One of the needs which educators have identified is that of providing a more economical and efficient means of distributing high quality learning materials to classrooms. Accessibility requires a means of transmission that provides for ready availability of the material. Is television the answer? As we consider the question of instructional television program material, further questions arise: Who will be the producers? Who will be the users? How are they related? Industry, although moving into education, has not produced a significant amount of learning materials in instructional television format. Instead, we have much in films, in transparencies and similar format. ITV is being widely used and its use is increasing, but effective formats for learning from television have yet to be developed.

52. American Film Institute. The American Film Institute's Guide to College Courses, 1969-1970. American Film Institute, Washington, D.C., 1969. (Available from American Film Institute, 1815 H Street, N.W.

Washington, D.C. 20006.)
An excellent guide for the educator who wants to know where courses in film and its uses are being taught. 219 higher institutions of learning have courses in film. 5300 students are preparing for a career in film production, scholarship or teaching.

53. Beck, Lester F. Educational Media for the Preschool Child. Monmouth, Oregon State System of Higher Education, 1965.

The philosophy and content of eight educational TV series for the preschool child are described by the people who created them. Illustrated by excellent photographs. The papers of this report indicate the direction that preschool ETV may take in the future, and is taking.

54. Costello, Donald P. A Memo on Film. ED 020 165; not available in hard copy. Order from EDRS, 4926 Fairmont Avenue, Bethesda, Md. 20014.

Written in response to inquiries from Upward Bound Project directors. Brief discussions and selected references for instructional use of films, types of films and availability and sources.

55. Costello, Lawrence F. and George N. Gordon. Teach with Television: A Guide to Instructional TV. (Communications Arts Books) Hastings House, 1961.

Instructional television, as defined by the author, is simply an attempt to teach in a formal manner over television at any level of schooling. The book discusses a specific course of study conceived for broadcast. It presents the experiences of many who are familiar with the problems involved in teaching with television. It treats both closed-circuit and standard broadcast.

56. De Korte, D. A. Television in Education and Training: A Review of Developments and Application of Television and Other Modern Audio-visual Aids. Philips Technical Library, 1967.

Translated from the original edition printed in Dutch by Elseviers Publishing Company, Amsterdam. A general view of the development and possible scope of television as well as other modern audiovisual aids. Includes a survey (1967) of developments in fields of educational radio and television in countries which are active in the field. Emphasis on educational television in the U.S. Includes programmed learning and teaching materials.

57. Department of Audio-Visual Instruction, National Education Association (now Association for Educational Communications & Technology). A Survey of Instructional Closed-Circuit Television, 1967. National Education Association, 1967.
A volume marking a decade of interest and leadership in educational television by the NEA and its DAVI. A survey which also includes 2500 ITFS facilities. The purpose of these research studies is to encourage the use of CCTV-ITFS as technical tools which can play an enormous role in improving the quality of instruction.

58. Diamond, Robert M. A Guide to Instructional Television. McGraw-Hill, 1964.
A broad reference source on instructional television, discussing uses of television in education, with emphasis on elementary and secondary levels. Points out effectiveness and efficiency of teaching in the classroom as it is increased by television. Several authors. Included here for its historical significance.

59. Educational Media Council. New Relationships in Instructional Television. Proceedings of the conference jointly sponsored by the Educa-Section of the Electronic Industries Association and the Instructional Division of the National Association of Educational Broadcasters in cooperation with the Educational Media Council, April 18-20, 1967. Educational Media Council, 1969.
The importance of this conference was its contribution to the effort to find new and better ways of serving the educational community through development of the EMC's own forum and dissemination functions. Educational television as an educational medium can be at once informative, challenging, significant and entertaining.

60. Giannetti, Louis D. Understanding Movies. Prentice-Hall, 1972.
A text on filmmaking which covers picture, movement, editing and sound as well as the art of the film in drama, literature and theory. It is well-illustrated and will be a good background text for the teacher of film production.

61. Gilliom, Bonnie Cherp. ITV: Promise Into Practice, by Bonnie Cherp Gilliom and Anne Zimmer. Ohio Department of Education, 1973.
The role of ITV in education is emphasized here, not television as an added part of the curriculum. The book

stresses local production by schools and school districts. A practical book putting ITV in perspective. Also available through ERIC.

62. Giraud, Chester. Television and Radio, by Chester Giraud, Garnet A. Garrison and Edgar E. Willis. Appleton-Century, 1963.
Television and radio in society and in the studios. Training students in broadcasting skills and supplying them with a body of knowledge about the field. The book is included for historical value.

63. Gottesman, Ronald. Guidebook to Film, by Ronald Gottesman and Harry M. Geduld. Holt, Rinehart and Winston, 1972.
An exhaustive collection on the making of film; contains books, periodicals, listings of schools, equipment and supplies, distributors, organizations and services, festivals, awards and terminology.

64. Hoffer, Jay. Organization and Operation of Broadcast Stations. Tab Books, 1971.
An excellent discussion of film study from the standpoint of teaching and learning. It emphasizes that traditional educational materials must incorporate the use of media to enhance the learning process and to meet the changing needs of students and teachers.

65. Hood, Stuart. A Survey of Television. William Heinemann, 1968.
Based on the author's experience in executive positions in both the British Broadcasting Corporation and Independent Television, this survey gives achievements and shortcomings of the industry. A history of television in Britain.

66. Huss, Roy. The Film Experience, by Roy Huss and Norman Silverstein. Dell Publishing Company, 1968.
Principles and techniques to increase the viewer's enjoyment and understanding of motion pictures. A good book which discusses the film experience, continuity, rhythm, imagery, tone and point of view as well as theme.

67. ITFS: What It Is ... How to Plan. Editor, Bernarr Cooper. The Division of Educational Technology, National Education Association, for the FCC Committee for the Full Development of the Instructional Television Fixed Service. National Education Association, 1967.

The Federal Communications Commission in October, 1965, established a national Committee for the Full Development of the Instructional Television Fixed Service, to meet the need and demand for information concerning the service and need for coordination in making efficient use of available frequencies. The information is published under the auspices of the Committee. It consists of basic information, planning and preparation in getting started, basic technology and means of estimating cost of equipment. The book contains an excellent bibliography on the subject of instructional television fixed service.

68. Judy, Stephen. A Study of the Production and Use of Videotaped Materials in the Training of In-Service and Pre-Service Teachers of English. Illinois State-Wide Curriculum Study Center in the Preparation of Secondary Teachers (ISCPET), Urbana, 1969.
Available from EDRS, ED 030 671, or in hard copy. An excellent study showing effective use of television with the videotape recorder.

69. Lewis, William C. Through Cable to Classroom: A Guide to ITV Distribution Systems. Edited by Harry T. Engle. National Education Association, 1967.
The book stresses the design of the instructional system. In the case of television, this means information about both its technical capabilities and its instructional application. DAVI (now AECT) reports on new directions in the field of educational television and communications.

70. Liebert, Robert M. The Early Window: Effects of TV on Children and Youth, by Robert M. Liebert, John M. Neals and Emily S. Davidson. Pergamon Press, 1973.
The authors make a clear case for the value and power of educational television in this carefully researched book. They emphasize the power television has in teaching and modifying behavior.

71. McBride, Wilma. Inquiry: Implications for Televised Instruction. DAVI (AECT), Center for the Study of Instruction, National Education Association, 1966.
Contains two excellent papers on the uses of educational television and the school curriculum. Discusses systems structuring and teaching and learning with the inquiry method. Examines the implications of inquiry for design and structure of television-learning programs.

72. MacLean, Roderick. Television in Education. Methuen Educational, Ltd, 1968.
    An account of current developments in Britain, including articles which appeared in the Times Educational Supplement. Discusses television in the single school, in teacher training, in the universities, the teacher and producer, as well as area closed-circuit systems.

73. Maynard, Richard R. The Celluloid Curriculum: How to Use Movies in the Classroom. Hayden Book Company, 1971.
    Specifically a discussion of the use of film in the classroom in pursuit of standard educational objectives. The author is from an inner-city school. The book is a practical guide to the use of films in the classroom; it is one of a series, the Hayden Film Attitudes and Issues Series, by the same author.

74. Millerson, Gerald. The Technique of Lighting for Television and Motion Pictures. Hastings House, 1972.
    A good resource book for those who work with television lighting. Well-illustrated, comprehensive, in a readable style.

75. Moir, Guthrie, ed. Teaching and Television: ETV Explained. Pergamon Press, 1967.
    The book surveys the use of television in schools in Great Britain. It is a progress report covering ten years of achievements.

76. National Association of Educational Broadcasters. Improvement of Teaching by Television. Proceedings of the National Conference of the National Association of Educational Broadcasters, University of Missouri, March 2-4, 1964. Edited by Barton L. Griffith. University of Missouri Press, 1965.

77. Oringel, Robert S. For Radio and Television Broadcasting. Hastings House, 1972.
    This latest (4th) edition of a familiar resource book in broadcast audio control is completely rewritten to include more information on the technical and electronic aspects of audio operation.

78. Postlethwait, S. N. The Audio-Tutorial Approach to Learning. 3rd edition, by S. N. Postlethwait, J. Novak and H. T. Murray, Jr. Burgess, 1972.

Provides an excellent description of the audio-tutorial system, an instructional method used in many schools today, particularly in science and laboratory classes. The book discusses the potential of mini-courses, problems a student faces when he enters an individualized study program. The authors do point out the limitations of the method of study; often those who use the system do not ask questions that should be asked or do not determine alternatives.

79. Reid, J. Christopher and Donald W. MacLennan. Research in Instructional Television and Films. U.S. Department of Health, Education and Welfare, Office of Education, 1967.

A report of some 350 research studies concerned with instructional television and film, done before 1967. Summaries prepared by the authors are well-organized for use by school administrators, curriculum directors and media specialists.

80. Routt, Edd. The Business of Radio Broadcasting. Tab Books, 1972.

For the radio station manager. Discusses radio facility operation in detail. The general purpose of the book is to integrate the concepts of radio broadcasting management principles, public relations, policies, legal interpretations, federal politics and "to interpret the everyday operating problems of commercial radio for practical operation."

81. Thornton, James W. New Media and College Teaching, by James W. Thornton, Jr., and James W. Brown. Department of Audiovisual Instruction (now AECT), NEA, 1968.

A comparison with a publication of five years ago, New Media in Higher Education, shows that most obvious changes have been quantitative and in new relationships between men and machines. Machines in themselves are the least important aspect of technology. The primary concern is in new relationships with clearly thought-out objectives. This book is written by the directors of the Higher Education Media Study; the two volumes, this and the one five years ago, make available a comprehensive fund of information and insights on contemporary use of new media technology in higher education.

82. Wade, Serena E. The Effect of Different Television Utilization Procedures on Student Learning. EDRS, 1968.

This is available in both hard-bound copy and microfilm from EDRS. A good research study supporting the use of television in the classroom.

83. Wagner, Richard V. and others. A Study of Systemic Resistance to Utilization of ITV In Public School Systems, Vol. I and II. American University, 1969. Available from EDRS in hard copy.
   The objective of this study was to identify and describe problems experienced by public school systems in increasing utilization of instructional television (ITV) subsystems. The second volume is a collection of case studies; it is also available in hard copy from EDRS.

84. WGBH Educational Foundation. The ITV Humanities Project: A History of Five Experimental Programs for Instructional Television. WGBH Educational Foundation, 1968. Available from EDRS or in hard copy.
   From many proposals studied in 1967, the ITV Humanities Project selected five instructional television series proposals which show an innovative, interdisciplinary approach to teaching humanities in the high school. These were selected to be developed as pilot productions. The report is of real value to the administrator or media specialist interested in producing instructional television programs.

85. White, David. The Celluloid Weapon: Social Comment in the American Film, by David White and Richard Averson. Beacon Press, 1972.
   A chronologically organized listing of more than 700 titles of American theatrical films. These are films which in the judgment of the writers "deal with specifiable social issues." The book is further evidence that film and television do have significant effects on human behavior. The book points out that the film is excellent background for such critical considerations as: Are film, television and audio and videotape recordings weaponry in controlling social thought? Are we really sure of our democracy and its identity?

86. Wigren, Harold E. Using Instructional TV: Elementary, Kindergarten and Nursery Education, available from National Education Association, No. 282--8854.
   School television can relate our courses to the business of life. Television can help us to bring a new sense of meaning and relationship to the knowledge we acquire.

Instructional television (ITV) is invaluable to the elementary school teacher, according to this small leaflet which contains many valuable ideas.

87. Woolman, Lorraine. <u>The Effect of Video-Taped Single Concept Demonstrations in an In-Service Program for Improving Instruction.</u> Houston University, Texas Bureau of Educational Research and Service, 1969. Also available ED 032 771.

  A convincing argument for the use of video-tape demonstrations in the classroom. The study is one of the best in the use of video-tape in classroom situations.

Chapter 5

PROGRAMED INSTRUCTION

The introduction to "Trends in Instructional Technology, 1970, the ERIC at Stanford 1970 Planning Report" states: "American education is under such pressure today, and the problems facing it will require such a massive infusion of national responsibilities and enlightened action, that every possible solution needs to be investigated. This report is on the determination of these trends in instructional technology."

The publication stresses the progress that has been made in individualization of instruction, as exemplified in programed instructional techniques, which are considered to be the predominant contribution of instructional technology during the past few years and which have significant implications for future education. Outstanding among the outcomes of this experience is the tendency to establish measurable behavioral objectives or goals, the assessment of results and the increasing attention given to the characteristics of the learner as they relate to means of teaching and forms and materials of teaching.

C. Ray Carpenter, writing on the accomplishments of instructional technology in the same publication, states, "I feel good about the effects, the residue of programmed instruction ... the effects on an increasing number of people of emphasis on the need to specify learning objectives." He remarks about the emphasis on individual learning but stresses the need for social contingencies, social requirements and socially motivated factors to accompany learning today.

It is agreed by most participants in the advisory council concerned with the ERIC publication that programmed instruction is an educational landmark. Many see more evaluation occurring in the future of the functional results and operations of the total instructional systems--including cost-effectiveness, performance measures, the investigation of areas that now defy adequate evaluation, and measures of individual learning as related to specific educational objectives.

But all who are involved in use of instructional technology in education today see that there must come increased emphasis on the production of instructional materials. Previous research in programmed instruction, in individual programmed instruction, is very valid here. Specific suggestions are for more open-ended materials, the developing of materials for existing equipment, new forms and formats, and new materials concerned with social action and the student.

88. Bjerstedt, Ake. <u>Educational Technology.</u> Halsted Press, John Wiley and Sons, 1970.
  A survey of programed instruction--history, development, state of the art at the time. Valuable to the appreciation and evaluation of every conceivable approach to programing and when selecting formats appropriate to many types of program objectives. Sections are basic principles of instructional programming, system analysis, system synthesis and techniques of system modification. Good organization.

89. Calvin, Allen D. <u>Programmed Instruction: Bold New</u>

Venture. Indiana University Press, 1969.
This is one of the "Bold New Venture" series, designed to inform educators about new developments and innovations in education and to assist in their evaluation. The contributors of these books are practitioners. Pitfalls are exposed; candid treatment is given to the issues. Today's teachers must act. Educators must leap from theory to practice in individualizing instruction. This book focuses on the practical problems of teaching.

90. deCecco, John P. Educational Technology: Readings in Programmed Instruction. Holt, 1964.
A good collection of knowledgeable authors who discuss theory and practice of educational technology, stimulus factors, response mode, knowledge of results and learning objectives, consideration of individual differences, evaluation and school use. Lawrence M. Stolorow writes the paper on implications of current research and future trends. Although ten years old, it is included here for its useful background information.

91. Dunn, W. R. Aspects of Educational Technology. Proceedings of the Conference on Programmed Learning and Educational Technology held at the University of Glasgow, April 5-8, 1968; edited by W. R. Dunn and C. Holroyd. Methuen, 1969. 2 vols.
These books contain papers presented before the conference and include topics on basic research and presentation systems; applications of programmed learning in schools and in higher education. Papers were presented covering aspects in other countries, relating educational technology to industry, to medical education. Many speakers discuss the possibilities of computer-assisted instruction and the role of the computer in educational libraries.

92. Fry, Edward B. Teaching Machines and Programmed Instruction: An Introduction. McGraw-Hill, 1963.
A good text for courses dealing with audiovisual education. It discusses the machine, principles of programming, educational objectives and uses of programmed learning. The book contains a good chapter on judging programmed instruction quality. Included in this bibliography because of its basic information, despite its early date.

93. Fund for the Advancement of Education. Four Case Studies in Programmed Instruction. The Fund, 1964.
Programmed instruction in Manhasset Junior High

School, in Denver, and in the Chicago area, plus a paper on programmed instruction today and tomorrow by Wilbur Schramm are included. The conclusion is that only a tiny fraction of the potential of programmed instruction is being realized. Emphasized is the need for research toward larger implications and imaginative applications of programmed instruction by the schools. Principles of programmed instruction can be applied to all educational media.

94. Garner, Wayne Lee. Programed Instruction. Center for Applied Research, 1966.

A comprehensive history of programed instruction and its use as a functional educational tool. Surveys of educational research and discussion of selected applications of programed instruction as an element in educational systems are included. The new computers' use and implications for the future emphasize changes in educational facilities and in teaching and learning.

95. Glaser, Robert. Teaching Machines and Programed Learning, I and II: Data and Directions. Department of Audiovisual Instruction (now AECT), NEA, 1965.

Good articles by important writers in the field of programed learning and computer-based systems in education and psychology. Subjects discussed include perspectives and technology, analysis of instructional objectives, various subject areas and technology in teaching school use of programed instruction, in industry, in federal government agencies. The book has a good concluding section on instructional design. Note: A bibliography on programed instruction, by Robert Glaser and Mary Louis Marion, was commissioned and is available from the ERIC Clearinghouse, Stanford University.

96. Jacobs, Paul I. and Milton H. Maier, with Lawrence M. Stolorow. A Guide to Evaluating Self-Instructional Programs. Holt, 1966.

A handbook defining programed instruction with suggestions for a self-evaluation study of instructional systems.

97. Komoski, Kenneth. Programmed Instructional Materials for 1964-1965: A Guide to Programmed Instructional Materials Available for Use in Elementary and Secondary Schools as of April, 1965. Columbia University, 1965.

A subject bibliography listing 542 programed instructional units for elementary and secondary schools. Center for Programmed Instruction of Educational Technology, Teachers College, Columbia University.

98. Lange, Phil C. **Programed Instruction: 1967 Yearbook of the National Society for the Study of Education, Part II.**
    This yearbook is an excellent review of the past of the programming movement. It includes the foundations of programed instruction, its history and theoretical base. Section two reviews the theory and mechanics of program design, construction and evaluation. Section three discusses issues and problems confronting programmed learning. Administrative and curricular consideration, program production problems, application of programmed instruction in schools, machine teaching and future developments are discussed. The chapter on future development is of particular interest.

99. Lysaught, Jerome P. **A Guide to Programmed Instruction,** by Jerome P. Lysaught and Clarence M. Williams. Wiley, 1965.
    A concise guide to preparation of instructional materials. The book is, as well, a concise history of programed learning, written as an aid to teachers and training specialists. Discusses selecting a unit to be programed, appropriate objectives, constructing the program, editing and review of evaluation.

100. Mueller, Theodore H. **Proceedings of the Seminar on Programmed Learning,** edited by Theodore H. Mueller. Appleton-Century, 1968.
    The University of Kentucky, Twentieth Foreign Language Conference, Lexington, Ky., April 29, 1967. The complexities involved in programing for a foreign language were discussed. The pertinent question was to what extent a foreign language can be programed. The conferees discussed using programed instruction in language courses in college, interacting in a language program, problem areas in programed instruction for modern language learning, retention of programed instruction, problems in definition of learning, steps in programed foreign language materials, psychological aspects and much discussion of possible programing of foreign language instruction.

101. Pipe, Peter. **Practical Programing.** Holt, 1966.
    A small text on programed instruction which discusses its history, both linear and branching programing, preparation of a programed instructional program, details of writing the program, the importance of testing and revision and editorial qualities.

102. Roucek, Joseph S. Ed. Programmed Teaching: A Symposium on Automation in Education. Philosophical Library, 1965.

An important book for the teacher who is disturbed about the potential future effect of automation on the teacher and education. The book discusses the experiments and hopes related to automation in teaching. It discusses teaching machines, the effects of automated teaching on the classroom teacher and on teacher education, the programed textbook, automation of guided planned experiences in creative thinking, programing of teaching in humanities and social sciences, in the secondary school social sciences and in language arts. Several speakers are quoted on automation of teaching in special education. The book is aimed at the teacher and the general public.

103. Taber, Julian I. Learning and Programmed Instruction, by Julian I. Taber, Robert Glaser and Halmuth H. Schaeffer. Addison-Wesley, 1965.

The book discusses the history of programed instruction and its current development. It emphasizes that there is little substitute for research, development and demonstration. Emphasis on the importance of principles in developing programed instruction is technical and detailed.

104. Tobin, M. J. Problems and Methods in Programmed Learning; the Proceedings of the 1967 APL/NCPL Birmingham Conference, Part 3, edited by M. J. Tobin. National Centre for Programmed Learning, School of Education, University of Birmingham, England, 1967.

Of interest to educators, the book discusses programed learning at the primary age, school experiments in the use of programed tapes with the student teacher and in secondary subjects. It emphasizes the value of evaluation and control of programed classes in degree courses. The book is in mimeographed form.

UNPUBLISHED MANUSCRIPTS ON PROGRAMED INSTRUCTION

1. Fass, M. L. and Sherman, C. D. Self-Instruction for the Medical Student: Developments in Cancer Teaching. Paper presented at the meeting of the National Society for Programmed Instruction, Boston, April, 1967. Available from senior author: University of Rochester, Rochester, N. Y. 14627.

2. Feldhusen, J. F. The Right Kind of Programmed Instruction for the Gifted. Paper presented at International Meeting of the Council on Exceptional Children, Toronto, April, 1966. Available from author: Educational Psychology Section, South Courts, G, Purdue University, Lafayette, Indiana 47907.

3. Feldhusen, J. F., Starks, D. D. and Bell, N. T. Problems in Working with University Faculty and Graduate Students in CAI Programming. Paper presented at the meeting of the National Society for Programmed Instruction, Boston, April, 1967. Available from senior author, see previous reference.

4. Feldhusen, J. F., Starks, D. D. and Bell, N. T. Achievement, Attitudes, and Learner Characteristics in Adjunct Instruction. Paper presented at the meeting of the National Society for Programmed Instruction, April, 1966. Available from senior author, see previous reference.

5. Flynn, J. T. and Morgag, J. H. A Methodological Study of the Effectiveness of Programed Instruction Through Analysis of Learner Characteristics. Paper presented at the meeting of the Psychological Association, New York, September, 1966. Available from senior author: University of Connecticut, Storrs, Conn. 06268.

Chapter 6

COMPUTER ASSISTED INSTRUCTION

CAI, computer-assisted instruction, is defined as the use of high-speed computers in education, which, in general, reduce time to completion of a learning task. The use of other acronyms, including CBI, CNI, CAL and CAE, may confuse and mislead the reader, although all refer to various interactive uses of computers for instruction. CAI, adopted by IBM in their early writing about instructional systems, is probably the most common acronym. System Development Corporation and Stanford University, as well as RCA, have used the term CBI, computer-based instruction. The U.S. Naval Academy uses CAE, computer-augmented education. However, CAI is the term most generally accepted and used today. A list of definitions and references is available from the American Standards Association, 10 East 40th Street, New York, N.Y. 10016. A glossary of terms is available from the Superintendent of Documents, U.S. Government Printing Office, Washington, D.C.

The biggest barrier to CAI's widespread use is its prohibitive cost. A recent trend in application of the computer is computer-managed instruction, of which several examples are currently going on. They are designing learning interventions based on carefully specified behavioral objectives. The computer is used to mediate between the student,

Computer Assisted Instruction

his individual performance on the objectives and the inventory of instructional resources.

The U.S. Office of Education has sponsored projects on computer applications in education costing several million dollars (Morgan, 1968), projects which include investigations of computer-based guidance systems and flexible scheduling. Other agencies, including the National Science Foundation and the Department of Defense, have sponsored education-related studies with the computer. An ad hoc study group of the USOE was formed to determine what had been accomplished and what were the pressing priorities for future computer applications support. The consequences of this survey and analysis were that the Office of Education decided that one of its highest priorities would be to study the feasibility and desirability of supporting the establishment of a computer center for education. This program has been called "A Computer Utility for Educational Systems" (CUES), and two contracts were awarded for it--one of them to General Learning Corporation to study this problem and to make recommendations for an approach.

The flexibility of the educational system is the reason that much of the potential impact for instructional improvement through use of instructional technology is lost. An application of a systems approach to the redesign of a school's total educational program is exemplified in a cooperative program presently underway: "Educational Systems for the Seventies" (Morgan and Morgan, 1968). The U.S. Office of Education's Bureau of Research has joined with eighteen local high school districts in fifteen states to design and develop a new educational program. The "Educational Systems for the Seventies" schools have already agreed upon their broad aims (Morgan and Bushnell, 1967). But for these goals to become purposeful in a new system design they must be operatively defined in terms of behavioral systems. With performance objectives it will be possible to associate behavioral change with program cost. Student learning must be the basis upon which cost-effective analyses, a prime concern of the American taxpayer, are made in education. There must be careful and systematic planning.

The most complete review of computer-assisted instruction and of the educational applications of the computer has been done by Robert M. Morgan of Florida State University, <u>A Review of Educational Applications of the Computer, Including Those in Instruction, Administration and Guidance</u>, issued as a Series Two Paper by ERIC of Stanford, in August, 1969.

Several excellent reviews of the literature on computer-assisted instruction have been published in the last few years. The most recent position paper by John H. Feldhusen on CAI Research and Development was issued by ERIC at Stanford in February, 1970. Karl L. Zinn and Susan McClintock, Center for Research on Learning and Teaching, University of Michigan, in January 1970 issued the second edition of <u>A Guide to the Literature on Interactive Use of Computers for Instruction</u>, as a part of Project CLUE under U.S. Office of Education sponsorship (issued as a Series One Paper by the ERIC Clearinghouse on Media and Technology). Vinsonhaler at the Computing Center of Michigan State University maintains a computer listing of an annotated bibliography on computers in education. New editions are published twice a year; it is published under the sponsorship of MICIS (Michigan Inter-University Committee on Information Systems). Zinn works with U.S. Office of Education funds on an evaluative review of the interactive uses of computers in instruction. Project CLUE (Computer Learning Under Evaluation) will attempt to assess technology, applications, costs, effectiveness and trends for uses of computers in secondary and university instruction. The RAND study (Rand Corporation of Santa Monica, California) for the Kerr Commission on Higher Education, which is a study of the prospects for computer-assisted instruction in higher education, will be coordinated with the USOE study. The latest bibliography, by Richard E. Clark, The Best of ERIC: Recent Trends in Computer Assisted Instruction, published by ERIC in 1973, brings up-to-date the record of ERIC publishing in the field of computer-assisted instruction.

105. Association for Educational Communications and Technology. The Computer Speaks Out. AECT, 1973.
This bibliography brings together references on computer assisted instruction. It is well-indexed and is included here as supplementary to this section.

106. Atkinson, R. C. and H. A. Wilson. Computer-Assisted Instruction: A Book of Readings. Academic Press, 1969.
A good group of reprinted articles which discuss educational considerations, hardware, languages, and economics.

107. Barnes, O. D. A Computer-Assisted Instruction Annotated Bibliography. Phi Delta Kappan, 1968.
This well-selected bibliography of 113 articles is included here for its wide variety of sources. Gives the reader much background information on CAI which is not found in texts.

108. Bitzer, D. L. Some Pedagogical and Engineering Design Aspects of Computer-Based Education. University of Illinois, Computer-Based Education Research Laboratory, 1968. (Position paper, ASEE Symposium)

109. Briggs, L. J., Campeau, P. L., Gagné, R. M. and

May, M. A. Instructional Media: A Procedure for the Design of Multi-Media Instruction. A Critical Review of Research and Suggestions for Future Research. American Institute for Research, 1967.

The proposed solution to a long-standing problem for the audiovisual communication specialists--that of choosing the most appropriate medium for instruction from an ever-increasing number of audiovisual media of instruction--is the subject of this report. The solution ties the behavioral objectives to be taught with the eight types of learning identified by Gagne in his book, Conditions of Learning. The final chapters include a selective review of literature on audiovisual media of instruction, conclusions and recommendations.

110. Brown, G. W. Edunet: Report of the Summer Study on Information Networks Conducted by the Interuniversity Communications Council (EDUCOM), by G. W. Brown, S. G. Miller and T. A. Keenan. Wiley, 1967.

The resources of entire regions will be made available to enrich and individualize the program of each student, no matter where he is located. Computer-based networks will distribute interactive information-processing services which individual institutions and community education programs could not afford separately.

111. Bryan, G. L. Computers and Education. M. I. T. Symposium Series, 1968.

Outstanding papers on computer use in education; slightly out-of-date.

112. Bushnell, Don D. and Dwight W. Allen, eds. The Computer in American Education. Wiley, 1967.

An in-depth report of the state of the art of computer applications in education. Not really up-to-date in a field that is still changing and growing so rapidly, but it does identify a solid body of objectives and issues and examines developments to date and implications for the future. The book includes an extensive bibliography on educational data processing.

113. Carter, C. M. Costs of Installing and Operating Instructional Television and Computer-Assisted Instruction in Public Schools, by C. M. Carter and M. J. Walker. Booz, Allen and Hamilton, 1968.

An excellent comparative study of school districts which have operating systems, done commercially.

114. Clark, Richard E. The Best of ERIC: Recent Trends in Computer-Assisted Instruction. ERIC, 1973.
     This publication is divided into six sections: CAI Planning and Utilization; Case Studies; Attitudes Toward CAI--Students, Teachers and School Administrators; Cost-Effectiveness Studies; Research Trends and Future Prospects and Policy. It is an annotated bibliography consisting mostly of publications available through ERIC.

115. Coulson, John (ed.) Programmed Learning and Computer-Based Instruction: Proceedings of the Conference on Applications of Digital Computers to Automated Instruction. Wiley, 1962.
     Early background of the application of computers to instruction.

116. Coulson, John Computer-Assisted Instructional Management. System Development Corp. Document SP-3000, 1969.
     An up-dated review of applications of the computer to instruction.

117. Engel, Gerald W. Computer Assisted Instruction: A Selected Bibliography and KWIC Index. NWL Technical Report TR-2283, U.S.N.W.L., 1969.
     This bibliography was published in 1967 and revised in 1968 and 1969. It overlaps the ENTELEK bibliography but does include some annotations. The ENTELEK abstract card file is more extensive and includes longer annotations, but is available only by annual subscription.

118. Feldhusen, John H. A Position Paper on CAI Research and Development: with Abstracts of Selected CAI Papers, by Paul Lorton, Jr. A Series Two Paper from ERIC at Stanford, February, 1970.
     The author states his beliefs and biases and reviews several relevant papers. His paper contains recommendations for CAI systems, language, interface and program development. Most important are recommendations for CAI research. He states that some major systems problems should be solved. With some suitable equipment, systems and instructional software, he feels that CAI research can become more effective and begin to produce significant results.

119. Flores, Ivan. Computer Software: Programming

Systems for Digital Computers. Prentice-Hall, 1965.
This is an advanced programing book which examines the various kinds of software, discusses generally how they are used and observes the design principles employed in current and future systems. The author assumes a basic knowledge of programing but does provide some basic information for a programer entering the software field. The book presents, in detail, general principles applicable to all programing systems. A view of the whole field.

120. Gerard, R. W. Computers and Education: A Workshop Conference at University of California, Irvine, edited by R. W. Gerard and J. G. Miller. McGraw-Hill, 1967.
This conference organized by the University of California, with support from the Office of Education, explored the present realities and future opportunities for interweaving the new resources offered by computer systems with the educational, research, service and related goals of a newly emerging campus. It deals with learning aspects, technical aspects, library handling of books and their contents, stored information, administration and regional and national networks of computer-assisted instruction.

121. Goodlad, John I. and others. Computers and Information Systems in Education. Harcourt, 1966.
Discusses the routine uses of educational data processing for business and student accounting as well as innovative uses in instruction. A description of computers and electric accounting machines, and an evaluation of their potentials and limitations in a variety of school situations are included.

122. Gruenberger, Fred. Computers and Communications--Toward a Computer Utility, edited by Fred Gruenberger. Prentice-Hall, 1968.
Essentially this book is the proceedings of a symposium held in March, 1967, jointly sponsored by the University of California at Los Angeles and Inmatics, Inc. This was the fourth such forum on information processing. Brings together the thinking of pioneers and leaders in timesharing communication, computer utility concepts, the role of the computer in education, medicine, governmental services and business. There is a need to understand the potentials and problems of the computer utility.

123. Hickey, Albert E., ed. Computer-Assisted

Instruction: A Survey of the Literature, 3d ed. Entelek, Inc., 1968.
References to literature published on computer-assisted instruction before July, 1968 are presented in nine subject areas.

124. Hicks, Bruce L. The Teacher and the Computer, by Bruce L. Hicks and Stephen M. Hunka. W. B. Saunders, 1973.
Written for the teacher, this would be a good text in CAI courses. It contains discussions and illustrations of aspects of instruction with the computer and CAI environments.

125. Holtzman, Wayne H., ed. Computer-Assisted Instruction, Testing and Guidance. Harper, 1970.
The glories of machine-made education are presented in this symposium of 25 papers from a University of Texas conference. For the academic or research-oriented library.

126. Holznagel, Donald. Computer Education Resource Catalog. Computer Instruction Network, 1968.
A detailed catalog of sources in computer education, published periodically, which includes a serial bibliographic listing of books, pamphlets and periodicals in general categories according to their major content or purpose, an annotation of certain of the works, and a listing of films and reviews.

127. Institute for Development of Educational Activities. Proceedings of Project ARISTOTLE Symposium. National Security Industrial Association, 1969.
The meetings of Project ARISTOTLE (Annual Review and Information Symposium on the Technology of Training, Learning and Education) in December, 1967, included a session on use of computers in education. Copies of the Proceedings are available from the National Security Industrial Association, Suite 800, 1030 15th Street N.W., Washington, D.C. 20005.

128. Lekan, Helen, ed. Index to Computer Assisted Instruction. University of Wisconsin-Milwaukee: Instructional Media Laboratory, 1969.
A comprehensive bibliography of over 450 entries encompassing 37 subject areas. It includes a detailed description of each entry, additional sources to consult, and

four major areas of cross references. Second edition forthcoming from Sterling Institute, Washington, D. C.

129. Markle, D. G. The Development of the Bell System First-Aid-and-Personal Safety Course: An Exercise in the Application of Empirical Methods to Instructional System Design. American Institutes for Research, 1967.
This study employed a mix of tailored media which underwent three revisions based on learner data. While this study is not conclusive, it does suggest that more effective instruction can be developed even without the computer.

130. Molnar, Andrew and Beverly Sherman. U. S. Office of Education Support of Computer Activities. U. S. Government Printing Office, 1969.
A volume of reports, project abstracts and various appendices related to the U. S. Office of Education support of computer activities in instruction and research (January, 1969). A five-page summary of the report appears in the April, 1969 issue of Educational Technology.

131. Morgan, Robert. A Review of Educational Applications of the Computer, Including Those in Instruction, Administration and Guidance. ERIC Clearinghouse on Educational Media and Technology, 1969.
A comprehensive and up-to-date review of educational applications of the computer; the Richard E. Clark publication from ERIC, 1973, supplements and brings this earlier review up-to-date. See entry no. 114.

132. Rosenbaum, J., Samuel L. Feingold, Charles H. Frye and F. D. Bennik. Computer-based Instruction in Statistical Inference, Final Report. Systems Development Corporation, 1967.
A report based on experiments. Computation is such an obvious application that it tends to be overlooked by the planner of a computer-based instructional system.

133. Sippes, Patrick. "On Using Computers to Individualize Instruction," in Don D. Bushnell and Dwight W. Allen, The Computer in American Education. Wiley, 1967.
Much of this same information is also contained in an article in Scientific American, 215 (3):207-220, 1966. Of especial interest to schools planning programs of independent study.

134. Stolorow, Lawrence. "Computer Based Instruction," in The Schools and the Challenge of Innovation. McGraw-Hill, 1969, pp. 270-319.
This was also issued as Supplementary Paper No. 28 of the Committee for Economic Development. It details computer uses in school administration and curriculum.

135. Uttal, William, Timothy Pasich, Miriam Rogers and Ramelle Hieronymous. Generative Computer-Assisted Instruction. University of Michigan, Mental Health Research Institute, Communication, No. 243, 1969.
An earlier Uttal publication, Real-Time Computers: Techniques and Applications in the Psychological Sciences (Harper & Row, 1969) is basic to this publication.

136. Vinsonhaler, John. Index for Bibliography of Computer Applications in Education. Michigan State University, Information Systems Laboratory, 1968.
A contribution to the literature in the field of computer-assisted instruction.

137. Zinn, Karl L. "Computer Assistance for Instruction: A Review of Systems and Projects," in Don D. Bushnell and Dwight W. Allen, The Computer in American Education. Wiley, 1967.
An excellent review, a second edition of which was completed in January, 1970, with Susan McClintock. See next entry.

138. Zinn, Karl L. and Susan McClintock. A Guide to the Literature on Interactive Use of Computers for Instruction, 2nd ed. Issued as a part of Project CLUE, U.S. Office of Education, as a Series One paper, ERIC Clearinghouse on Educational Media and Technology at the Institute for Communications Research, Stanford University.
Provides a list of information sources, a glossary of terms and a list of typical projects. An important contribution to any independent study program of the future.

Chapter 7

DESIGN AND PRODUCTION OF INSTRUCTIONAL MATERIALS

The design of the instructional materials involves the whole concept of the learning resources center. Media, in whatever form, should be viewed, first, for their informational or motivational use; and secondly, for their format. The filmstrip may be a better source of information on a specific subject than the book.

The design of instructional objectives is the concern of both the teacher and the librarian. The library traditionally supplies and supports through selection, evaluation, distribution/retrieval, description and storage of nonprint and print materials. Hardware (equipment) systems serve a teaching function and must be considered in design. Appropriate learning models to meet individual needs are the goal of the library media center or resources center. The learning center can be what the institution determines it to be.

The learning resources center should provide for the production of materials for instruction by both teachers and students as well as by the center itself. The student in the library media center often turns to the library for creative projects or programs supplemental to his educational program, or for creative interests and needs.

The 1969 Standards for School Media Programs of the American Library Association and the National Education Association recommend that the center offer services to

Design and Production of Materials

assist teachers, students and technicians to produce materials which supplement those available through other channels or in the collection of the center. Production equipment and materials needed include (per building): dry mount press and tackling iron, paper cutters, two types of transparency production equipment, 16mm. camera, 8mm. camera, 35mm. still camera, rapid process camera, equipment for darkroom, spirit duplicator, primary typewriter, copy camera and stand, light box, film rewind, film splicer (8mm and 16mm) tape slicer, slide reproducer, mechanical lettering devices, portable chalkboard. It is recommended in the Standards that the staff assume responsibility for production of materials, television and radio programs, electronic banks of materials, museum services, as well as study guides necessary for their proper and full utilization.

Peggy Sullivan, writing in Problems in School Media Management (R. R. Bowker, 1971), discusses some of the problems of reproduction services, including teachers' rights to ideas in materials duplicated by request, handling of requests for materials to be produced, taping (video, audio) of teacher and student presentations and the form needed for the release of such presentations, taping of visiting speakers, decisions regarding duplication of materials from a department, materials that are technically poor, differences in formats, center policy regarding number of copies to be made, and formats to be used. These are only a few of the practical problems the media center director or librarian must face and resolve.

Those who work with students in the library media center or in the university library know that it is an important principle of education that what people do effects change in their behavior. If students are to learn skills they must be given opportunities, that is, the tools required for learning must be at hand and they must be helped to use such tools and materials wisely. They must be led to the facts relevant to the experiences leading to problem solutions. Thus, it is most important that the library work with the teacher in specifying instructional objectives and selecting content and methods to be used.

The production function of the learning resource center must be adapted not only to the center's needs but should be coordinated with production facilities elsewhere in the school or campus. Most college and university media preparation services fall short of satisfying or supporting the needs of various programs.

139. Arrasjid, Harun and Arrasjid, Dorine A. Media: a Pocket Guide. MSS Educational Publishing Company, 1970.
 For the teacher, users of machine laboratories and beginning teachers this is a good guide which provides comprehensive information about all forms of instructional media. The format is convenient for reference. Contains exhaustive lists of uses, advantages and disadvantages as well as discussions of operations, care of equipment and causes of difficulty.

140. Brown, James W. and Richard B. Lewis. AV Instructional Technology Manual for Independent Study. McGraw-Hill, 1973.
 A step-by-step manual for choosing, using and producing instructional materials, and for operating audiovisual equipment. It contains a section on the development of independent study packages. Particularly suited to independent study and the contract method of teaching. Planned to correlate with AV Instruction: Technology, Media and Methods, by James W. Brown, Richard B. Lewis and Fred F. Harcleroad, 4th edition, 1973. See entry no. 155.

141. Calder, Clarence R. Techniques and Activities to Stimulate Verbal Learning, by Clarence R. Calder,

Design and Production of Materials

Jr., and Eleanor M. Antan. Macmillan, 1970.
This excellent book describes and details a great variety of approaches to stimulate teachers to develop other avenues of learning. Part II gives techniques for creating many instructional materials and is concerned with the development of production techniques. Part III focuses on instructional tools. An excellent source list of tools and materials is included.

142. Eastman Kodak Company. Movies With A Purpose. Eastman Kodak Company, n. d.
Well-illustrated and practical, this publication for the professional library collection stresses production within the school. A valuable instructional reference on filmmaking.

143. Frye, Roy A. Graphic Tools for Teachers. 3d edition. E & I Printing Company, 1965.
A manual of conventional as well as recent educational media. The author calls it a selective manual but it is fairly inclusive. It does emphasize use of the overhead projector, and rightly so, as this is the media projection machine which requires the greatest knowledge of educational graphics. Sections include lettering, mounting, types of overhead projection, as well as the making of transparencies and slides for projection. There is a good section on sources of materials and equipment.

144. Garvey, Mona. Teaching Displays: Their Purpose, Construction and Use. Linnet Books, 1972.
A handbook to help teachers develop display ideas and techniques which can be applied to any subject at any level.

145. Goudket, Michael. An Audiovisual Primer. Teachers College Press, 1973.
A beginner's guide to the production of useful classroom AV materials. Problems of presentation, repair, sources and information, and production methods are clearly presented in a non-technical manner.

146. Horn, George F. How to Prepare Visual Materials for School Use. Davis Publications, 1963.
A collection of visual aid techniques useful for instruction. Suggestions for professionally prepared educational media and discussions of techniques that can be easily utilized and perfected by the teacher are included. Emphasis is on teacher-prepared visual material.

147. Kemp, Jerrold E. Planning and Producing Audiovisual Materials, by Jerrold E. Kemp with the assistance of Ron Carraher and Willard R. Card. Chandler, 1968.
   Important for its emphasis on the preparation of instructional materials to meet specific needs within the school and classroom. It discusses why you should prepare your own materials and how to get started. The philosophy is more important than the ways to prepare the materials. An excellent book for the school media director or administrator looking for and introducing the use of new educational materials. The fundamental skills discussed are many and include all media. A fine addition to the collection on educational media in the professional library.

148. Kuhns, William and Thomas F. Giardino. Behind the Camera. Pflaum, 1970.
   A valuable book for the teacher or media specialist interested in filmmaking with a class or student group. This very detailed book is, in fact, a diary of all that went into the making of a student film, including instructions on how to purchase a camera, learning to film with video tape, and an annotated bibliography of 18 books.

149. Lynch, Helen C. Handbook for Classroom Videotape Recording. Southeastern Educational Corp., n.d.
   A brief and thorough guide for making more effective use of the videotape recorder and player in classrooms to improve instruction.

150. Minor, E. and Frye, H. Techniques of Producing Visual Instructional Media. McGraw-Hill, 1970.
   A well-illustrated and excellent book for use with teachers in the professional library or with a college class on production.

151. Pearson, Neville P. Instructional Materials Centers: Selected Readings, by Neville P. Pearson and Lucius Butler. Burgess Publishing Company, n.d.
   Included here because it points out the need for a production center in the library media center. An excellent collection of readings describing and advocating the design of instructional materials centers to meet the needs of today's schools.

152. Schultz, Morton J. The Teacher and the Overhead Projector. Prentice-Hall, 1965.

Design and Production of Materials

Written for the educator who wants to learn about uses for the overhead projector. A complete description of the various types of equipment and materials available, uses and capabilities. A treasury of ideas, uses and techniques.

153. Thornton, James W. New Media and College Teaching, by James W. Thornton, Jr., and James W. Brown. American Association for Higher Education; Department of Audiovisual Instruction, 1968.

Five hundred current innovative media projects in 300 colleges and universities are reported here by faculty members responsible for them. Reports are arranged by fields and present valuable creative ideas for design and production of educational media materials.

154. University of Texas. Local Production Techniques. Visual Instructional Bureau, University of Texas, n. d.

Prepared by Ernest F. Tiemann and revised by Richard E. Smith, this simply written book for the classroom teacher discusses dry mounting, laminating, color lifts, lettering and projection.

Chapter 8

PRE-SERVICE AND IN-SERVICE
TRAINING OF TEACHERS

J. Robert Oppenheimer wrote almost twenty years ago (in <u>Perspectives, U. S. A.</u>, 1955), "This world of ours is a new world, in which the unity of knowledge, the nature of human communities, the order of society, the order of ideas, the very nature of society and culture have changed, and will not return to what they have been in the past.... One thing that is new is the prevalence of newness, the changing scale and scope of change itself, so that the years of a man's life measure not some small growth or rearrangement or modernization of what he has learned in childhood, but a great upheaval!" And think how things have changed since then!

Marshall McLuhan wrote, in <u>Understanding Media: The Extensions of Man</u> (McGraw-Hill, 1964), that change is an "implosion which is all-at-once, instantaneous, all-encompassing and inevitable.... The vehicles of this titanic event are the electronic machines and communications devices of today and there is no turning back--we must continue to hasten along the ever-steeping spiral of change."

This is the world for which we must educate our children--not the comfortable predictable world of the Greek city state but a dynamic electronic world of ever-increasing change. In fact, we have to educate them for a world that does not exist, that is in the future.

One hopes that the concept of teacher as kindly philosophical scholar guiding students is not lost; the human touch is still as necessary as ever. But the teacher of today needs at hand the latest and most effective tools which modern technology can supply--the media that are going to confront our children all their lives. The modern teacher, too, must employ the methods of analysis and synthesis which have produced travel to the moon or made it possible for man to live for 84 days in space.

The role of the teacher must become that of the guide to the means and sources of education, a selector of processes and experiences for the student. His role is no longer that of the all-knowing source of knowledge and experience. He must still be an adult model for the student, but he must approach the student as an individual, not a member of a class or group. Electronic teaching techniques, systematic instruction and electronic processing devices are means to assist in the individualization of instruction for a larger numbers of students, with superior results. The use of newer tools and newer methods will more adequately fit our children to live in tomorrow's world.

Educational training should equip an individual to make use of an extremely wide range of educational and communications media and to benefit from excellent counseling and guidance of wise instructors. The learner must be capable of orienting himself to a changing world. The development of the individual is our goal and purpose. The student should be taught to question but to base questioning on the best available information and experimentation. His search should be for truth.

It is the exceptional educator who has begun to use new

media and has developed techniques in teaching, learning and research which adequately "program" technology into his teaching. Use of media and a systems approach to teaching through planning and experimentation are needed as we look to the future of the students in our class and consider our ability to prepare them for the world of tomorrow.

155. Brown, James, W., Richard B. Lewis and Fred F. Harcleroad. <u>A-V Instruction: Media and Methods</u>. 4th edition. McGraw-Hill, 1973.
   A valuable reference book for anyone in the media field, this fine revision includes much pertinent research and survey data which has previously been available only in scattered and specialized sources. Useful as a text, reference or self-instruction manual, it includes newer kinds of educational media and improved techniques. Also included are the uses of a systems approach to education, the use of multi-media kits, individually prescribed instruction, CAI, the use of the portable taperecorder (VIDEO) and a radically revised section on programed instruction. The emphasis is on clarification of objectives, strengths of a particular teaching staff, and suitability of media and evaluation. A fine text for the prospective teacher or a resource item for the teachers' library in the school.

156. Cook, Myra B., Joseph H. Caldwell and Lina J. Christiansen. <u>The Come-Alive Classroom: Practical Projects for Elementary Teachers</u>. Parker Publishing Company, 1967.
   A cross-section of practical classroom projects, gathered from 20 different classrooms--the best ideas, projects and philosophies of twenty teachers from kindergarten through college. Many educational media are described. A fine book on uses of instructional media in the classroom.

157. Cullum, Albert. <u>Push Back the Desks</u>. Citation Press, 1967.
   This exciting book is a sensitive, creative approach to the problem of learning in the classroom, written for the elementary teacher. Creativity, activity, eagerness, energy and independence--all imply the excitement of uses of varied media.

158. Dale, Edgar. Audio-visual Methods in Teaching. 3rd edition. Holt, Rinehart and Winston, 1965.
The basic text for audiovisual theory. Part I, Theory of Audiovisual Instruction, deals with the widely known "Cone of Experience." Parts II and III cover actual classroom applications of audiovisual instruction. It is a total revision of the earlier work.

159. de Kieffer, Robert E. Audiovisual Instruction. The Center for Applied Research in Education, Inc., 1965.
An excellent contribution to the literature on educational media, this book deals with designing schools for the use of audiovisual materials, research in educational media, a discussion of audiovisual materials and their use, including both projected and nonprojected materials. It discusses equipment and administering the audiovisual program. The book is a very complete volume and gives an excellent view of how education may be improved through the use of modern means of teaching and learning.

160. de Kieffer, Robert E. and Lee W. Cochran. Manual of Audio-Visual Techniques. Second edition. Prentice-Hall, 1963.
This manual is designed to be used alone or with other AV texts and sources. It emphasizes learner involvement to develop the techniques and skills needed in the effective utilization of instructional materials in the classroom.

161. Erickson, Carlton W. H. Administering Instructional Media Programs. Macmillan, 1968.
A book for professional use and for graduate student study. Comprehensive in scope, it deals primarily with technological media, discussing the complexity that has developed in the field. Particularly noteworthy are bibliographies, questions, problems and references. The book's unique organization contributes to its use. Audio-visual media are emphasized although no de-emphasis of print media is intended by the author. It is an attempt to deal with audio-visual media service problems and discusses administration, media preparation, services, instructional systems, budgeting, public support and evaluation.

162. Firth, Brian. Mass Media in the Classroom. Macmillan, 1968. (Macmillan, Ltd., London)
Relates the teacher's responsibility to the individual pupil to his responsibility for guiding pupils in their virtually involuntary roles as recipients of mass-communications.

Each teacher must learn from his own experience what he can accept and what he must reject from mass media. It is an honest study of some media and an excellent statement of principles and problems of mass-communications. Media discussed are: newspapers, magazines, television, advertising, film, all with interesting comments by Raymond Williams and Marshall McLuhan and recommendations of other writers on media.

163. Hanna, Paul R. Geography in the Teaching of Social Studies: Concepts and Skills. Houghton, 1966.
One section of this book, Aids for Teaching, is an excellent source of ideas for multi-media teaching in the social sciences.

164. Herbert, John David. A System for Analyzing Lessons. Teachers College Press, Columbia University, 1967.
In the introduction, in which the author discusses teaching, he distinguishes between general methods and special methods, by which he means "audiovisual methods." Ways of teaching in Chapter 2 and in the book as a whole stress a systematic approach to teaching and planning. The use of the simplest appropriate media is recommended.

165. Homine, Lloyd E. A Demonstration of the Use of Self-Instruction and Other Teaching Techniques for Remedial Instruction of Low-Achieving Adolescents in Reading and Mathematics. TMI Institute, Albuquerque, New Mexico, n. d. (Available from ERIC Document Reproduction Service, No. ED 018 111.)
Included here because it points out the necessity for communication. The failure of a classroom experiment in programmed instruction scheduling because of lack of communication among experimenters, teachers and administrators is discussed in this paper.

166. Jarvis, Oscar T. The Transitional Elementary School and Its Curriculum, by Oscar T. Jarvis and Lutian R. Wootton. Brown, 1966.
Section Three of the book shows how the elementary teacher, equipped with a knowledge of the school's function in our society and an understanding of children, uses this information for effective teaching. Various types of instructional media are set forth as instruments for learning which the teacher utilizes in problem-solving procedure. A good basic book for the educator considering the addition of various media to the school media center's basic collection.

Training of Teachers   61

167. Joyce, Bruce R. Man, Media and Machines: the Teacher and His Staff. National Commission on Teacher Education and Professional Standards, NEA, 1967.
   The author describes new and different roles for the competent and imaginative teacher, unusual ways of using many resources. The Direct-Instruction Team and Support Teams, including the computer-support center, self-instruction center, inquiry center, materials creation center--all are discussed. The book discusses the independent study approach to learning as well as group-inquiry. It is a forward-looking view of school organization and new media use.

168. Kent, Graeme. Blackboard to Computer: a Guide to Educational Aids. Ward Lock Educational, 1969.
   A recent book surveying uses of many educational media in England. It emphasizes uses made of teaching aids and stresses that there is nothing difficult or puzzling about educational technology. It is a combination of a teacher's craft with any implements he or she uses. No two teachers are alike and no two teachers will use teaching aids in the same fashion. Basic aids are discussed and evaluated as well as CCTV. The author states "educational technology will accomplish exactly what the teacher wants it to accomplish--the tools are there."

169. Kinder, James S. Using Audio-Visual Materials in Education. American Book Company, 1965.
   An excellent orientation to uses of audio-visual materials in education. A flexible text which would serve for in-service education as well as for a short course. The first chapter, "Today's AV Materials," discusses education and technology and their relationships. Chapter seven discusses newer educational media, ITV, the language laboratory and programed learning.

170. Mills, Belen C. and Ralph A. Mills. Designing Instructional Strategies for Young Children. William C. Brown, 1972.
   A book for the new or in-service teacher offering new views of teaching. The Decision-making Process, Understanding the Teaching-Learning Process, Strategies for Teaching, Combining Strategies for Individualized Instructional Programs, and The Process of Evaluation--are the five sections of the book. Recommended as a textbook for courses dealing with educational designs, methods and construction of these designs. Good self-evaluation guide.

171. Thomas, Murray and Sherwin G. Swartout. *Integrated Teaching Materials.* Revised edition. David McKay, 1963.

   A basic audiovisual text included here because of its value for pre-service and in-service training of teachers. It points out the importance of local production of teaching materials. It also recognizes the importance of printed materials in the classroom and discusses their selection and utilization. The appendices include source lists for films, records and textbooks.

172. Torrey, George N. *Instructional Media: Theory-Application,* by George N. Torrey and Richard P. Finn. Kendall/Hunt Publishing Company, 1971.

   A practical manual covering most of the commonly used audiovisual materials and techniques, which can be used as a laboratory workbook, an in-service manual or a supplementary text. For each medium discussed, their is a brief history, plus a discussion of operation of the device and software to be used. Good photographs and drawings. Not a self-instruction manual. Discusses several models of each machine.

173. Wittich, Walter Arno. *Audiovisual Materials: Their Nature and Their Use.* Fourth edition, by Walter A. Wittich and Charles Francis Schuler. Harper, 1967.

   A valuable contribution of this text is the discussion of educational media and their use. Early chapters discuss the teacher and the communications revolution, learning and communications and the research basis for teaching with many educational media. It is a good text which contributes many worthwhile ideas to the teacher in the classroom, and to the university and college teacher as well.

Chapter 9

ADMINISTRATION OF EDUCATIONAL MEDIA

The media program in a school includes all of the media services to the school, the administration of the collection, and uses of media, both book and nonbook materials. All are coordinated in the library media center under the direction of the librarian or media specialist. To make effective use of media, whether in a school on the elementary or secondary level, or in the university, administration must be well-planned and coordinated. To effectively use materials they must be organized and cataloged. There must be a carefully planned and balanced program of learning resources. The concept of the media center or learning resource center provides for integrated use of all media. In education, the secondary schools have led the way in this approach to learning. Many of the community colleges are moving toward the concept of integrated media use, but the four-year program is changing more slowly, and in many colleges the audiovisual department is entirely separate from the library.

Edgar Dale has said that "every classroom can have the best in instructional materials now produced" ("Toward Excellence in Instruction," Audiovisual Instruction, September, 1973) but even if the school's instructional materials are less than excellent, they must be well-organized and administered for effective use. The library is the center of the program and must lead the way to effective use of educational media. A fine, attractive learning resources center is not the only answer. Teachers must be led to, informed about, and must make use of book and nonbook resources to be found in the center. The program of the media center must be planned also to meet the varying and different needs of students.

It is the responsibility of the school librarian or media specialist to formulate the objectives of the specific media program, the sum total of all services and learning involved in the center. This must be based upon full and effective participation in the school's curriculum planning. One objective must be to stimulate and guide students and teachers in the uses of media. Another of the objectives of the media center must be to provide the opportunity for creative uses of media, to recommend and suggest to students appropriate uses of all media as they work in the center or library.

It is necessary that teachers be involved in the selection of media as well as in utilization. To effectively use media as an integral part of the classroom instruction, teachers must know what is available, have previewed the materials, and have access to the needed equipment and materials. Most of the media program will be implemented outside the center itself, to facilitate and enrich the instruction in the classroom.

"The educational program of the school is strengthened in direct proportion to the quality of the school's library service," said the 1960 Pennsylvania Governor's Committee on Education. The statement is as valid today as it was then. Today the media specialist or librarian is a teacher

Administration 65

in the best sense of the word. His responsibility extends far beyond organizing and maintaining a materials collection. He works directly with teachers and students to achieve educational excellence.

174. American Association of School Librarians and the Department of Audiovisual Instruction. Standards for School Media Programs. ASCD-DAVI, 1969.
In order to create and maintain adequate media standards, it is necessary to refer to an ideal media program that is generally adaptable. Specific desirable acquisitions, requisite school facilities and desirable supplemental programs are discussed.

175. Association of Supervision and Curriculum Development, 1965 Yearbook Committee. Role of Supervisor and Curriculum Director in a Climate of Change; prepared by the ASCD 1965 Yearbook Committee, Evelyn F. Carlson, chairman; edited by Robert R. Leeper. ASCD, NEA, 1965.
The book concerns itself with changes in curriculum and the means of meeting those changes. Chapters on the emerging role of the curriculum leader and on the future of the climate of change are excellent.

176. Bailey, Catherine M. Educational Communications Handbook. New York State Education Department, Division of Educational Communications, Albany, 1968.
An overview concerning staff, school facilities, educational equipment and materials necessary in instructional programs.

177. Brown, James W. and Kenneth D. Norberg. Administering Educational Media. McGraw-Hill, 1973.
One of the best in educational media administration, this book is the first to consider the subject in all of its modern aspects. Media specialists and general administrative officers with responsibilities for developing and organizing technological resources will find it very useful. Included are policy guidelines and detailed practical and technical information at several administrative levels.

178. Brown, Louis H. A Study to Determine the Feasibility

of Developing a Coordinated Distribution System for Audio-Tape Recorded Materials. Available from ERIC, ED 018 109, 1969.

This specific study is applicable to much of media administration. It includes reports and data on tape use and distribution derived from questionnaires sent to all U. S. audio-tape libraries in public, private and "progressive" schools (50 percent were returned). Recommendations are made for establishing a model for a national tape distribution system with autonomous regional centers.

179. Erickson, Carlson W. H. Administering Instructional Media Programs. Macmillan, 1968.

An excellent text which will be useful for the media program director and for the school administrator. The author discusses all media and their application to the school's instructional program. The aim of the author is to stimulate creative decision-making in organization and implementation of media programs of wide application. Nonprint media are emphasized although print media are also discussed. In-service education is also emphasized.

180. Iowa State Department of Public Instruction. Plan for Progress in the Media Center. ISDPI, 1969.

The outpouring of new instructional materials and techniques has resulted in a demand for media centers at the elementary level. This handbook has been published to assist in planning and developing such a facility. Guidelines for materials, space, service, equipment and budget are included.

181. McGowan, William N. New Directions for School Administration. California Association of Secondary School Administrators, 1969.

A general discussion of the many changes in secondary education, with particular emphasis on information systems, computer-assisted instruction and use of data processing in school management.

182. Sullivan, Peggy. Problems in School Media Management. Bowker, 1971.

The second book in the case study series, Problem-Centered Approaches to Librarianship, this one concerns itself with the school library media center. Miss Sullivan, from her experience with the Knapp School Library Project in high schools across the country, writes and devises case studies which deal with the problems of today's school librarian and media specialist. The cases are well-chosen, although at times a little too detailed to bring out the point of the problem. It is a good, readable book for addition to the collection on administration of educational media in the school. Many cases can be applied to all levels of instruction.

183. Wilkinson, Cecil E. Educational Media and You. Silver Burdett, 1971.
A comprehensive book covering all media, traditional as well as "newer." Advice on effective and efficient utilization of media is included, as well as technical information. Good chapters on development of the media program, administering media programs, and facilities for such centers. It uses a case study method to present tried and proven techniques, not just theory. The author is well-qualified and presents a practical approach to educational media use, distribution and administration.

184. Wyman, Raymond. The IMC--Whose Empire? Department of Audiovisual Instruction, National Education Association, 1967.
Points the way to service in the library media center and suggests that the three elements needed are: 1) software for media library; 2) hardware or equipment; and 3) production center for preparation of instructional materials.

Chapter 10

MEDIA IN CURRICULUM DESIGN

There are a variety of definitions of educational technology or educationa media. The Random House Dictionary defines technology (educational technology) as "The application of knowledge to practical ends, as in a particular field: educational technology." The U.S. Office of Education has established a National Center for Educational Technology. In our schools and libraries we are most concerned with media, many resources which are used in teaching and learning. Hence the name educational media.

The Department of Audiovisual Instruction (now AECT) Commission on Definition and Terminology has this definition: "Educational technology is that field of educational theory and practice primarily concerned with the design and use of messages which control the learning process." The term audiovisual communication was the label formerly used (in 1963).

The Presidential Commission on Instructional Technology (Report of the Commission on Instructional Technology to the President and Congress of the United States, U.S. Government Printing Office, 1970) offers the following: "Educational technology is a systematic way of designing, carrying out and evaluating the total process of learning and teaching in terms of specific objectives, based on research in human learning and communication, and employing a combination of human and non-human resources to bring about more effective instruction."

Whichever definition is chosen, the important aspect is that education is a systematic process within the framework of educational technology or educational media, a process with a purpose. The purpose of curriculum design is to bring about more effective learning, to solve educational problems, to design effective instruction. Curriculum development must be systematic if students are to learn to the maximum. We are a goal-oriented society. Whereas most curriculum planning has traditionally been concerned with content, design for learning in the classroom and school today is based upon objectives. Educational technology is concerned with curriculum design emphasizing objectives, as well as with methods, materials and evaluation. A. Maugham Lee, writing in Audiovisual Instruction (Vol. 16, No. 10, December, 1971), states that "Instructional development seems to hold the greatest promise yet for a way to improve instruction and promote more efficient learning in our increasingly complex and technological society, and without compounding the very problem that we are trying to solve."

The purpose of design as a function is to translate general educational technology theory and research, as well as subject-matter content, into specifications for learning resources. Design is not as broad a term as development; development includes production and evaluation functions as well as design.

Students enjoy mediated instruction; they do learn and their varying needs can be met through the use of many media. But media must be a part of planned instruction, and we must have clearly stated objectives.

This bibliography emphasizes the importance of design in the curriculum, and the place media has in learning in our schools. We will "manage" learning as we consider planning, controlling, organizing and uses of media. It is the teacher and his new concept of teaching and learning that will change education. It is not the machine but how and why media are used that is important.

184. Arrasjid, Harun. Media Objectives for Teachers. MSS Educational Publishing Co., 1971.
An excellent handbook with clearly stated instructional objectives related to instructional media and materials. Specific pages are referred to in widely used media textbooks. The author believes that a system should incorporate media usage to achieve a maximum level of learning performance. He discusses media objectives in all situations--large group, small group and individualized instruction.

185. Axeen, Marina E. Teaching Library Use to Undergraduates--Comparison of Computer-based Instruction and the Conventional Lecture. Final Report. Illinois University, 1967. ERIC Document 014 316.
The overall objective of this study was to provide basic specific information concerning the effectiveness of computer-based instruction in teaching the use of the library. The conclusions drawn included: 1) students made significant gains in their knowledge of library use under both treatments; 2) the experimental and control groups did not differ significantly in the amount of knowledge gained as a result of their respective treatments. The study is included here for its applicability to other areas of teaching.

186. Bloodworth, Mickey. Highlights of Schools Using Educational Media, by Mickey Bloodworth and Desmond Wedberg. AECT (Association for Educational Communications and Technology), 1973.
This guide to educational practices in 247 school districts is a source for many innovative ideas and programs.

187. Brown, James W. and Thornton, James W. New

Media in Curriculum Design   71

Media and Higher Education. Association for Higher
Education and the Division of Audio-Visual Instructional Service, NEA, 1963.
   The premise of this book is that potential solutions
to the problems now confronting higher education will be
found within the fields of the new media. Chapters are included on administration and on instructional aims and new
media--both areas which need further exploration in higher
education.

188. Carnegie Commission on Higher Education. The
      Fourth Revolution: Instructional Technology in High
      Education. A report and recommendations by the
      Carnegie Commission on Higher Education. McGraw-
      Hill, 1972.
   It is the concern of the Commission report that
universities do not place the responsibility for instructional
technology high enough on the administrative ladder to ensure its effectiveness. The Carnegie Report is carefully
considered and realistic, and is based on a sophisticated
knowledge of management and finance. Regional and national
activities are recommended, as is extensive funding by the
national government. It is an excellent brief and readable
summary of the state of the art. The section on libraries
and the information revolution is of value.

189. Davies, Ivor K. The Management of Learning. Mc-
      Graw-Hill, 1971.
   The book is extensive, covering planning, controlling, organizing and use of media in instruction by the teacher. Good introductory chapters on the history of instructional technology, systems theory. Planning is discussed in
terms of task and skill analysis and objectives. There are
three chapters on measurement, evaluation and objectives.
Basically, the book is based upon research rather than personal opinion. Diagrams, charts and summary tables are
used extensively. An excellent book for graduate education.

190. Dwyer, Francis M. A Guide for Improving Visualized
      Education. Learning Services, 1972.
      Researchers will find this summary of some 32
studies an interesting guide to the potential of the picture as
an instructional medium.

191. Gerlach, Vernon S. and Ely, Donald P. Teaching
      and Media: A Systematic Approach. Prentice-Hall,
      1971.

Discusses the systematic approach to teaching and presents case studies. Part II discusses the role of objectives in learning. There is a good brief section on designing instruction. The rule prevailing in all areas of the book is: a medium of instruction must be selected on the basis of its potential for implementing a stated objective. Sources, references and bibliographies at the end of each chapter are excellent. One of the most practical and logical publications in the media field.

192. Lieberman, Irving. A Working Bibliography of Commercially Available Audio-visual Materials for the Teaching of Library Science. University of Illinois Graduate School of Library Science, Occasional Paper No. 94, 1968.

A selective, non-evaluative bibliography of films, filmstrips tapes and non-projected graphics. Includes annotation, distributor, price, LC card number and EFLA number when found in the bibliographic source searched.

193. McClosky, Mildred G. Teaching Strategies and Classroom Realities, ed. by Mildred G. McClosky. Prentice-Hall, 1971.

A practical, up-to-date book for the classroom teacher, and an excellent addition to the teacher's library in the school. Contains 91 articles by junior and senior high school teachers, describing their best learning experiences.

194. Schueler, Herbert. Teacher Education and New Media. American Association of Colleges for Teacher Education, 1967.

An introductory chapter discusses competencies required in a teacher. The book emphasizes uses of media in teacher education programs and their functional characteristics. Media research is reviewed and possibilities for new media in teacher education are considered. New media are considered primarily as a means, as instruments. The conclusion reached (applicable to all that a teacher will do in the classroom) is that consideration of media for research, for evaluation and for use must be based on their contribution to the outcomes of teaching.

195. Thornton, James W. New Media and College Teaching, ed. by James W. Thornton and James W. Brown. Department of Audiovisual Instruction (now AECT), Association for Higher Education, National Education Association, 1968.

Since the publication of New Media in Higher Education, five years previously, the most obvious changes have been in new relationships between men and machines. Machines in themselves are the least important factor; the primary concern must be new relationships between men and machines to accomplish clearly thought-out objectives.

196. Van Hoffman, Nicholas. The Multiuniversity: A Personal Report on What Happens to Today's Students at American Universities. Holt, 1966.

On the basis of first-hand knowledge, the writer tells what one university is like to the people who live in it. He includes reactions of students--the feeling of anonymity, etc. The book is based on personal observation and is included here as it points to ways in which we can improve teaching through uses of new media.

Chapter 11

INSTRUCTIONAL SYSTEMS ANALYSIS, DESIGN AND DEVELOPMENT

Literature abounds today with statements about systems thinking, the systems approach and systems analysis. The systems approach began with the development of weapons systems in the military and, in more modern times, with commodities in industry. In these areas it has been remarkably successful. The systems approach is a management tool which allows for examination of all aspects of a problem, to formulate a procedure using all resources at hand and to interrelate the effects of one set of decisions and another. The application of the systems approach in education may lead to a number of outcomes, but the principal objective in education is learning experiences that are better than have previously been the case.

Concerning such an approach to education, William Clark Trow (Teacher and Technology: New Designs for Learning, Appleton-Century-Crofts, 1963) states,

> A systems approach implies careful study of the treatment (input) required by each student, and the time when it is needed, in order to obtain the objective sought. Systems analysis is the comparison of alternate means of carrying out some function, where the means are complicated and comprise a number of interrelated elements.
>
> The new media will not be particularly effective as

Instructional Systems Analysis

long as they remain mere adjuncts, an intrusion, a fifth wheel of the educational conveyance. The new parts need to be integrated into a man-machine system, and this requires clearcut readjustments in organizations and procedure.... The educational technologist envisions not machine-produced robots, but a smoothly functioning system in which the several processes it employs are all operating to turn out its product ... and that product is educated people.

A few more statements may help define what a systems approach means. Leonard C. Silvern ("Reply to Questions about Systems," Audiovisual Instruction, Vol. 10, No. 5, May, 1965) says that "A system is the structure or organization of an orderly whole, clearly showing the interrelationship of the parts to each other and to the whole itself.... Through experience, I have found that the most critical aspect of system is the key word interrelationship.... A systems approach to any real-life problem is the application of analysis and synthesis to an instructional system."

Henry Lehmann ("The Systems Approach to Education," Audiovisual Instruction, Vol. 13, No. 2, February, 1968) states: "The systems approach does provide an orderly process for developing a solution, a process which is structured to minimize prejudicial preconceived notions, and maximize the objectivity required to arrive at a scientifically correct answer."

Steps which can be used to arrive at a framework for a systematic approach to education, no matter at what level of education, are considered here. The first step is to determine whether an educational need exists. If it does, educational objectives must be outlined. This is the key to the whole process and the hardest for most people to accomplish. Too often, we simply describe the course or lesson, without setting up the objectives against which students can be evaluated later.

Next, the situation in which the system will operate must be planned. The physical environment must be considered--the classroom, lighting, seating, etc.; the social and psychological environment--the inputs, what the learners will be like, their knowledge level, how many students, the available sources and procedures for developing suitable mediated materials; the required output--that is, how the objectives will be achieved and how to tell whether or not they are achieved; and finally, the internal balance of the system. Then a trial system is created, utilizing media, independent study, practice or review, contact in small groups--whatever is chosen to maximize learning.

There must be continuing feedback and modification, and this is where many schools fall down. Modification to assure continued responsiveness is the hallmark of a useful systems approach. Change is needed not only in what the student learns but in the structure and thrust of our educational institutions. We must teach people to learn--to continue to adapt through the conscious process of study if they are to survive in this world.

197. The Affective Domain, A Resource Book for the Media Specialist. National Special Media Institute, 1970. (Available from Gryphon House, Washington, D.C.)
Seven different authors present at least seven diverse viewpoints, but all show a concern for developing instruction which interests, involves and motivates learners. Seven facets of human feeling, or affect, are presented by authors who have been engaged in basic research and instructional applications of that particular approach. A useful book for the instructional technologist involved in designing, developing, or revising instructional systems, and of interest

to anyone concerned with improvement of instruction. Each chapter presents the approach and background of the problem, examples of the research and developmental studies, and implications for instruction.

198. Baker, Robert L. and Shutz, Richard E. Instructional Product Development. Van Nostrand Reinhold Co., 1971.

A beginning volume on instructional development; includes such areas as stating educational outcomes, constructing objectives of cognitive behavior, developing instructional specifications, educational criterion measures, rules for the development of instructional products, preparing instructional materials (products) and managing classroom contingencies. A good basic volume.

199. Banathy, Bela H. Instructional Systems. Fearon Publishers, 1968.

Develops a model for systematic instructional development. A fine reference source on systematic instructional development.

200. Barson, John. Instructional Systems Development. A Demonstration and Evaluation Project. U.S. Office of Education, Title III-B Project OE-3-16-025, Michigan State University, 1967.

Included here as a model--tested in a two-year study in instructional development in four institutions of higher learning (M.S.U., University of Colorado, Syracuse University and San Francisco State College)--for systematic development of college-level courses.

201. Bloom, Benjamin S., Taxonomy of Educational Objectives, Handbook I: Cognitive Domain. Longmans, Green, 1956.

This older classic on instructional objectives is a basic book for any collection on instructional design and development. It describes six levels of cognitive instructional objectives in terms of their nature, utility and measurement.

202. Briggs, L. J., Campeau, P. L., Gagné, R. M., and May, M. A. Instructional Media: A Procedure for the Design of Multi-Media Instruction, A Critical Review of Research and Suggestions for Future Research. American Institute for Research, Pittsburgh, 1966. (Available from librarian, American Institutes for Research, 135 N. Bellefield Avenue, Pittsburgh, Pa.)

A useful book for an overall view, with ideas for (then) future research, some of which have already been accomplished.

203. Bushnell, Don D. The Automation of School Information Systems. Monograph 1, Department of Audiovisual Instruction, N.E.A., 1964.
   One of a series of DAVI monographs, this brings together a wide range of school applications for automation. The emphasis is on electronic data processing for school administration and for retrieval of educational information, although it also discusses computer-based instructional systems, research in automatic teaching, and systems design and analysis for the university and the school.

204. Cook, Desmond L. Program Evaluation and Review Technique Applications in Education. U.S. Government Printing Office, 1966.
   Concerned with PERT and its use in facilitating the economical management of research and development projects in education. Discusses the management process, basic characteristics of PERT, and its application and implementation in educational projects.

205. Edling, Jack V. Individualized Instruction: A Manual for Administrators. DCE Publications, Waldo Hall, Oregon State University, Corvallis, Oregon, 1970.
   A reference source on individualized instruction, prepared for leaders in instruction such as principals, team leaders and curriculum directors. Section III contains chapters on instructional and evaluation procedures, problems and solutions, and recommended implementation procedures. A practical book.

206. Edling, Jack V. Individualized Instruction Case Studies. Institute for Communication Research, Stanford, California, 1970.
   A total of 46 case studies prepared for the administrator to use with the lay public. Questions are asked about program objectives, instructional procedures, results of the program, costs and problems. These are useful studies for teachers and curriculum directors.

207. Edling, Jack V. Individualized Instruction Slide-Audio Tape Sets. Available from AECT, 1201 Sixteenth Street, N.W. Washington, D.C.
   An excellent resource for in-service or

Instructional Systems Analysis

administrative institutes. The Manual and Case Studies (nos. 205 and 206 above) are correlated with them.

208. Gage, Gerald. A Model for Establishing a Priority of Educational Needs. Teaching Research, Monmouth, Oregon.
    A brief discussion of educational needs and their identification. It examines the sources for identifying needs, the determination of need values, and a need-value model for establishing a priority of needs.

209. Gagné, Robert M. The Conditions of Learning. Holt, Rinehart, 1965.
    Topics covered include: learning and the content of instruction, motivation, learning decisions in education, and resources for learning. The chapter on resources for learning is of value to anyone attempting to identify significant research questions. Media for instruction are emphasized; modes of instruction, tutoring sessions, lectures and recitation are also discussed.

210. Gagné, Robert M. Psychological Principles in Systems Development; foreword by Arthur W. Melton. Holt, 1965.
    A discussion of the interrelation and interdependence of psychological principles in the design of systems. By an authority in the field.

211. Gerlach, Vernon S. and Ely, Donald P. Teaching and Media: A Systematic Approach. Prentice-Hall, 1970.
    A guide and a handbook, as well as a collection of case studies. Discussed are selection and utilization of material to achieve classroom teaching/learning objectives, the design, implementation and evaluation of instruction around teaching media, and a point-by-point listing of the advantages and applications of all types of media. Sections are included on cognitive, affective and motor skill development.

212. Glaser, Robert, editor. Teaching Machines and Programed Learning, II: Data and Directions. National Education Association, 1965.
    This collection of key papers leading to the development of programed learning also contains and integrates "less current and comprehensive reports." Much wider in scope and depth than Volume I. The four sections include discussions on: 1) research findings on instructional

programs; 2) programed instruction in five subject areas; 3) implementation of programed instruction; and 4) a behavioral science base for instructional design. A significant contribution for instructional system designer.

213. Gronlund, Norman E. Stating Behavioral Objectives for Classroom Instruction. London: Macmillan Limited, 1970.
One of the best books on learning outcomes of general instructional objectives; the selection of appropriate objectives, relating them to classroom instruction and using them in test preparation. A concise and clear book.

214. Haga, Enoch. Automated Educational Systems. Business Press, 1967.
Potentialities for improvement and administration of instruction are discussed. The author's aim is to give administration and education an overview of where we stand in implementing automated systems, and its relationship to instructional objective achievement.

215. Kemp, Jerrold E. Instructional Design, a Plan for Unit and Course Development. Fearon, 1971.
Points out needs for improvement of instruction and introduces the instructional design plan, based on systems approach. Each element mentioned in the instructional design is applied to subject matter topics in social studies, general science, vocational guidance and instructional technology. The author points out the need for a planning board, and for teamwork among curricular and subject matter specialists, learning theorists, testing and measurement specialists, administrators, media specialists, librarians, technician, aids, secretary and students. A good planning layout is included in the appendix. An excellent book in the educational media field.

216. Knowlton, James Q. "A Conceptual Scheme for the Audiovisual Field." Bulletin of the School of Education, Indiana University, Vol. 40, No. 3, May, 1964.
For the student of research in educational media this paper is a contribution which should not be ignored. The bibliography is a valuable list of references in communications research.

217. Learning Directory. Westinghouse Learning Corporation, 1970. 7 vols.
A comprehensive guide to teaching materials at all

levels; includes 205,000 print and non-print items. Included are materials for purchase, loan or rental, and free materials.

218. Loughary, John W. Man-Machine Systems in Education. Harper and Row, 1966.
   Deals with "the nature and application of computers, media technology, and systems technology as they pertain to the instructional, administrative, pupil personnel services and preparation of staffs for educational institutions...."

219. Mager, Robert F. Preparing Objectives for Programmed Instruction. Fearon Publishers, 1962.
   A brief (and early) self-instructional program, recommended as a first reading for anyone interested in instruction objectives. The author's aim is that readers will be able to identify objectives stated in performance terms, to identify the portion of an objective that describes minimum acceptable performance, and to select test items appropriate to given objectives.

220. New Spaces for Learning. Center for Architectural Research, School of Architecture, Rensselaer Polytechnic Institute, Troy, New York, 1966.
   A revision of the 1961 publication. Provides comprehensive guidance for the design and planning of media-oriented learning spaces--particularly medium and large group rooms. Important inclusions are a series of design studies and documentation of a case-study demonstration.

221. Popham, W. James and Eva L. Baker. Establishing Instructional Goals. Prentice-Hall, 1970.
   A book for pre-service and in-service which uses a self-instructional program format. Filmstrip-tape programs are available from Vimcet Associates, Inc., P. O. Box 24714, Los Angeles, Calif. 90024. Considered in the book are: how to select goals, how to state goals, and how to establish pupil performance standards.

222. Popham, W. James and Eva L. Baker. Planning an Instructional Sequence. Prentice-Hall, 1970.
   Self-instructional text which focuses on planning a series of instructional activities to promote learner attainment of explicit instructional objectives.

223. Popham, W. James and Eva L. Baker. Systematic

Instruction. Prentice-Hall, 1970.
An orientation to instruction for those preparing to be teachers. It is an introduction to the kinds of general instructional strategies and particular teaching tactics. May be used with the two self-instruction texts by Popham and Baker (see nos. 221 and 222 above).

224. The Psychomotor Domain, A Resource Book for the Media Specialist. National Special Media Institutes, 1971. Available from Gryphon House, Washington, D. C. 1971.
Physical activities of the body such as coordination, reaction time and muscular control are the concern here. Despite a long history of attention in the elementary schools, physical education areas and some vocational areas, many educators and researchers have ignored this area of knowledge. The philosophy of the psychomotor conference and institute was to probe this area of human behavior and to look for possible applications to learning and to teaching. A valuable book for the teacher or administrator developing instructional systems.

225. Saracevic, Tefko. Introduction to Information Science. Compiled and edited by Tefko Saracevic. Bowker, 1970.
The question answered is: "What was and is the work of information science all about?" The book is theoretical and experimental rather than practical, and consists of readings on the communication process, structure of information retrieval systems, indexing vocabularies, abstracting, bibliographic representation, organization of information stores, search procedures, dissemination. An excellent text.

226. Tansey, P. J. Educational Aspects of Simulation. England: McGraw-Hill Publishing Company, Ltd., 1971.
A complete reference book on simulation and gaming as these techniques relate to instruction. Chapters include discussions of programed non-simulation games, simulation in teacher education, simulation of international relations, simulation games, and simulation and media.

227. Voight, Ralph C. Invitation to Learning. Acropolis Books, Ltd., 1971.
Delineates the learning center concept of teaching, including inventory, academic, cooperative, fun, prescriptive, skill development, and project. Lists educational tasks,

materials and activities for each. Well-illustrated. Much is demanded in the way of audiovisual and learning resources for this approach to teaching and learning. Emphasized is the need for teacher cooperation with the media center specialist and librarian.

228. Weisgerber, R. A. ed. Developmental Efforts in Individualized Learning. F. E. Peacock Publishers, 1971.

Explores actual developmental classroom efforts in individualized learning, looking at current efforts on four levels: 1) national level (Project PLAN and IPI); 2) elementary and secondary; 3) higher education; and 4) the future of individualized learning.

229. Weisgerber, R. A. ed. Perspectives in Individualized Learning. F. E. Peacock Publishers, 1971.

Articles by a cross-section of experts on learning theory, individual differences, measurement and evaluation, educational objectives, teacher roles, learning activities, facilities, technology and computer systems. Each chapter is prefaced by an introduction by the author. The readings present an analysis of important educational components, selected factors underlying the process of individualized learning. The book is organized topically and moves from theoretical considerations toward an analysis of educational components.

Chapter 12

SYSTEM EVALUATION

Educational evaluation must be based upon definition. A precise use of terms must be arrived at before evaluation begins, or before the evaluative instrument is devised. The basic terms given here are from the Dictionary of Education (Good, Carter V., ed., Dictionary of Education, 2nd ed., McGraw-Hill, 1959).

> Checklist. A prepared list of items that may relate to a person, procedure, institution, building, etc., used for purposes of observation and/or evaluation, and on which one may show by a check mark or other simple method the presence, absence, or frequency of occurrence of each item on the list.
>
> Criterion (criteria, pl.). A standard, norm, or judgment selected as a basis for quantitative and qualitative comparison.
>
> Evaluative Criteria. 1) The standards against which a person or group or a procedure may be checked; 2) the factors considered by an accrediting agency in analyzing the status of an educational institution to determine whether it shall be accredited.
>
> Evaluative Method. The procedure in a study that has evaluation as its chief purpose and that in most cases includes some definite fact finding, through observation, and that involves the careful description of aspects to be evaluated, a statement of purpose, frame of reference, and criteria for

the evaluation, and the degrees or terms that are to be employed in recording judgments.

Inventory. In the field of evaluation, a test or checklist used to determine the subject's or examinee's ability, achievement, aptitude, interest, or likes, generally in a limited area.

Rating Scale. A device used in evaluating products, attitudes, or other characteristics of instructors or learners.

School Survey. A study or evaluation of a school, a school system, or any part thereof; may be fact finding, or may indicate the strong and weak features as judged by definite criteria; commonly concluded with suggestions for needed changes and/or recommendations for more desirable practices.

Standard. 1) A goal or objective or criterion of education expressed either numerically as a statistical average or philosophically as an ideal of excellence; 2) any criterion by which things are judged.

Librarians and teachers work together when selecting resources to support the program of the school. A librarian must be knowledgeable of the educational program of a school. This is a time-consuming task but important as one aims to provide educational media for the total school program. He must consult with the administration as well as with individual teachers; he must analyze course content and know textbooks well, and must know topics, strategies and activities to be included in each unit plan. He must know his students, their needs, interests, goals, abilities and concerns. He must match materials with needs; offer services designed to make those materials effective teaching resources in the school.

Evaluation involves definition, decision-making, values and criteria, administrative levels and the research model.

In any evaluation there must be respect for the truth and seriousness of purpose. Evaluation should identify weaknesses as well as strengths. To improve is the goal of evaluation.

Library evaluation is a necessary part of any evaluation of the school's program. One of the purposes of standards is for evaluation; they are criteria. The 1969 <u>AASL-DAVI Standards for School Media Programs</u> are the most recent authoritative standards for the schools. <u>Guidelines for Two-Year College Learning Resources Programs</u>, published in 1972 and prepared by the American Library Association (Association of College and Research Libraries), the American Association of Community and Junior Colleges and the Association for Educational Communications and Technology, are a significant breakthrough for libraries, because of their approach by program rather than facility and because of their joint sponsorship by three concerned organizations.

230. Bloom, B. S., J. T. Hastings and G. F. Madaus. <u>Handbook on Formative and Summative Evaluation of Student Learning.</u> McGraw-Hill, 1971.
    Intended primarily for present and future teachers, this book discusses the "state of the art" in learning evaluation. Subjects covered are: 1) purposes of evaluation and types of evaluation instruments; 2) evaluation problems likely to be encountered by teachers; 3) evaluation techniques for cognitive and affective objectives, and 4) evaluation systems. There are illustrations of objectives and testing techniques.

231. Frederiksen, Norman. <u>Proficiency Tests for Training Evaluation in Training Research and Education.</u> Robert Glaser, ed. John Wiley, 1965.
    A short essay of 23 pages discusses seven methods of training evaluation and their advantages and disadvantages.

232. Grobman, Hulda. <u>Evaluation Activities of Curriculum Projects: A Starting Point.</u> AERA Monograph Series

on Curriculum Evaluation, No. 2. Rand McNally, 1968.
A well-written article on evaluation presents an excellent discussion at both the conceptual and applied levels, with sections on sampling, scheduling and budgeting.

233. Kaufman, Roger A. Educational System Planning. Prentice-Hall, 1972.
Deals only with educational planning--defined as needs assessment and system analysis. This practical book has a glossary of terms and exercises at the end of each chapter.

234. Knirk, Frederick G. ed. Instructional Technology: A Book of Readings. Holt, 1968.
Although not specifically on the subject of evaluation, this collection of 31 articles provides a basis for understanding instructional technology--uses of instructional methods as they are integrated with the total program system. Characteristics of available audiovisual media and associated materials are examined, as well as the effects of media and materials on the economics of instruction. Contains a bibliography and subject index.

235. Lessinger, Leon. Accountability: Policies and Procedures, Learner Centered Management Support Systems, by Leon Lessinger, Dale Parnell and Roger Kaufman. Croft Educational Services, 1971. 4 vols.
A handbook which provides a systematic approach to accountability in a school system through the development of clearly defined policies and procedures. The systems approach to policy development is the important emphasis. A helpful guide for developing a working document for a school system.

236. Paulson, Casper F. A Strategy for Evaluation Design. Available from Teaching Research, Publication Secretary, Monmouth, Oregon, 1970.
Includes the following sections: 1) Purpose for evaluation; 2) Defining the evaluation content; 3) Information collection procedures; 4) Instrumentation; 5) Information processing; 6) Distribution of information; and 7) Evaluation as management methodology. This fine reference source includes a bibliography.

237. Stufflebeam, Daniel L. and others, eds. Educational Evaluation and Decison-Making. Phi Delta Kappan, 1971.

Discusses five areas of evaluation: definition, decision-making, values and criteria, administrative levels and the research model. It discusses ways to deal with problem-areas and develops a new definition and methodology of evaluation resulting from the assessment. It provides operational guidelines for implementing the proposed new approach.

Chapter 13

LEARNING THEORY

The items listed in this chapter deal basically with education and learning as related to educational technology. There are references which discuss the major theories of learning in the twentieth century. Emphasis is upon books which attempt to answer the question of what is known about the process of learning which can be used to design better education in our schools and for individual students. A good background reading before progressing to other books in the bibliography is Robert M. W. Travers' <u>Essentials of Learning: An Overview for Students of Education.</u> An excellent book of background readings which analyze selected factors underlying the process of individualized learning is R. A. Weisgerber's <u>Perspectives in Individualized Learning.</u>

An excellent film--which shows the work of Howard Kendler of New York University, Tracy Kendler of Barnard College, Kenneth Spence of the State University of Iowa, Harry Harlow of the University of Wisconsin and B. F. Skinner of Harvard--is <u>Learning about Learning</u> (30 min., 16mm. black and white, 1963). The film is available from State University Film Service, 1400 Washington Avenue, Albany, New York 12203. It shows the different strategies employed by these men in developing new theoretical concepts about man's ability to learn, and demonstrates the effect of their theories and work upon methods of instruction in schools and colleges.

Instruction and learning encompass many processes, many that are not included in learning theories specifically. Instruction involves such considerations as stimulating recall, guiding the learning, gaining and controlling attention, aiding remembering, providing feedback and assessing outcomes. Ultimately, it is the learner who performs such functions. Carefully designed combinations of media best serve the teacher and the school to achieve the kind of learning that is most effective.

Robert Glaser, in a number of reports issued through the Learning Research and Development Center, University of Pittsburgh, stressed the concept of learning as education for individuals. The University of Pittsburgh Learning Research and Development Center is an important source for up-to-date information on individualized instruction and learning.

In this bibliography, basic background readings on learning are included to provide students of education with an overview of current knowledge. Emphasis is upon research taking place in the field of learning, and the implications of that research for educational planning. The need for further research, as it affects knowledge in learning theory, is emphasized.

238. Association for Supervision and Curriculum Development. Nurturing Individual Potential: Papers and Reports from the ASCD Seventh Curriculum Research Institute, ed. by A. Harry Passow. ASCD, NEA, 1964.
A collection of papers on factors affecting the nurturing of individual potential, focussing on some significant influences not as yet adequately explored by curriculum

planners. It is the cumulative interaction of students, staff, content, method, resources, school and community and family relationships which directly affect the development of the individual's potential.

239. Berthold, Jeanne Saylor and Mary Alice Curran. Educational Technology and the Teaching-Learning Process: a Selected Bibliography. U. S. Department of Health, Education and Welfare, National Institute of Health, 1968.

   An excellent earlier bibliography on education and learning as related to educational technology. The sections on theoretical formulations and teaching-learning are especially good. Included are multi-media approaches, films and television, programed instruction and computer-assisted instruction.

240. Briggs, Leslie J., Peggie L. Campeau, Robert M. Gagne and Mark A. May. Instructional Media: A Procedure for the Design of Multi-Media Instruction, a Critical Review of Research and Suggestions of Future Research. American Institutes for Research, 1967. Also available from the ERIC Document Reproduction Service, Bethesda, Md.

   The authors deal with a problem which has long plagued audiovisual communication specialists: choosing the most appropriate medium for instruction from the ever-increasing output of audiovisual media of instruction. The authors' solution ties the behavioral objectives to the eight types of learning outlined by Gagné in his book Conditions of Learning (see entry no. 245). An excellent review of the literature on audiovisual media of instruction is included in the final chapters.

241. Bruner, Jerome. Learning about Learning: a conference report, edited by Jerome Bruner, Director, Center of Cognitive Studies, Harvard University. U. S. Department of Health, Education and Welfare, Office of Education, 1966.

   Results of the Working Conference on Research on Children's Learning, supported by the U. S. Office of Education through the Cooperative Research Program. A background series of papers on how children learn.

242. Bruner, Jerome. Toward a Theory of Instruction. Belknap Press, Harvard University Press, 1966.

   As our technology grows more complex in both

machinery and human organization, the role of the school becomes more central in society--hence the need for a theory of instruction utilizing many sequences and educational media. Dr. Bruner emphasizes that we get interested in what we get good at doing. We must be concerned with how energies can be cultivated in support of school learning.

243. Calder, Clarence R., Jr. and Eleanor M. Antan. Techniques and Activities to Stimulate Verbal Learning. Macmillan, 1970.
Included here because it presents a diversified study of techniques and creativity related to learning theory and instructional development. The environment, the classroom teacher and the learner are examined. Learning principles are discussed in relation to their effect on the whole learning process. Implementation is discussed, and directions are given for creating instructional materials and for the development of production techniques. The section on use of instructional tools is particularly good. A source list is also included in this stimulating book.

244. Dale, Edgar. Audio-Visual Methods in Teaching. 3rd ed. Holt, Rinehart and Winston, 1965.
A revised version of a book which has been the cornerstone of audiovisual theory for over twenty years. The "Cone of Experience" discussed in Part I, Theory of Audiovisual Instruction, is the most valuable part of the book. Emphasis is placed on building from "direct, purposeful experiences" toward the use of visual and verbal symbols in a concrete to abstract continuum. Parts II and III cover materials and classroom applications of audiovisual instruction. Recent developments are covered in this edition.

245. Gagné, Robert M. The Conditions of Learning. Holt, 1965.
A comprehensive answer to the question of what is known about the process of learning that can be put to use in designing better education. Gagné identifies eight classes or types of learning: 1) signal learning; 2) stimulus-response learning; 3) chaining; 4) verbal association; 5) multiple-discrimination learning; 6) concept learning; 7) principle learning; and 8) problem solving. He discusses each in detail, provides examples, and cites the work of learning theorists who have done basic research on each type of learning. The eight types of learning are then related to instructional design and decision-making in education. The chapter, "Resources for Learning," discusses media for instruction and

Learning Theory 93

various modes of instruction. Many learning theories are discussed.

246. Gagné, R. M., ed. Learning and Individual Differences. C. E. Merrill Books, 1967.
A report of a conference of leaders in the field of learning theory, concerned with the problem of using knowledge of learning to help different learners. Valuable for varying points of view.

247. Gattegno, Caleb. Toward a Visual Culture: Educating Through Television. Outerbridge and Dienstfry, 1969.
Included here because it examines perceptively and in depth the premise that a person learns more through visual approaches than through speech. The author claims that his book tries to establish criteria for asking the "right questions" in order to produce programs which will satisfy the true needs of growth.

248. Hilgard, Ernest R. A Basic Reference Shelf on Learning Theory. ERIC Clearinghouse on Educational Media and Technology, Stanford, Calif., 1967.
A brief paper on learning theory, with commentary by Dr. Hilgard from Theories of Learning, 3rd edition (next entry, on applicability of learning principles and theories to media study.

249. Hilgard, Ernest R. and G. H. Bower. Theories of Learning. 3rd edition. Appleton-Century-Crofts, 1966.
Theories associated with early twentieth century learning theorists Thorndike, Pavlov, Guthrie, Skinner, Hull, Tolman, Kohler and Freud are discussed. Current developments are included: functionalism, mathematical learning theory, information processing models and neurophysiology.

250. Hilgard, E. R., ed. Theories of Learning and Instruction. National Society for the Study of Education, 63rd Yearbook, Part I. Distributed by University of Chicago Press, 1964.
The theories of authors such as Bruner, Carroll, Gagné, Glaser, Lumsdaine, McDonald, Pressey and Pribram are discussed as they bear upon educational practice. Comments upon current developments in learning theory are of value.

251. Jones, J. C. Learning. Harcourt, 1967.
Designed for professional use by teachers. There are suggestions for further reading at end of each chapter. Chapters included are on verbal behavior and concept formation, retention, transfer, and complex behavior including skills and problem solving.

252. Taylor, Calvin W. Instructional Media and Creativity: the Proceedings of the Sixth Utah Creativity Research Conference, edited by Calvin W. Taylor and Frank E. Williams. Wiley, 1966.
The purpose of the conference was to convene a small group of highly competent researchers of creativity and educational media, to identify additional needed research on the relationship of instructional media and creative behavior in the schools.

253. Travers, Robert M. W. Essentials of Learning: an Overview for Students of Education. 2nd ed. Macmillan, 1967.
An excellent book which reflects trends in the professional literature of education, points to the great need for more knowledge of the learning process, and relates results of research to problems in education.

254. Travers, Robert M. W. Man's Information System. Chandler Publishing Company, 1970.
A controversial book as viewed by others writing in the field of instructional and learning theory. Travers describes research indicating that human beings process information relatively slowly. It is based upon his earlier writing and research.

255. Weisgerber, Robert A. Instructional Process and Media Innovation. Rand, McNally, 1968.
Education makes use of technology in the relationship of media to curriculum in acquisition of skills, concepts and understandings, in attitude development and creativity. The final section deals with the use of audiovisual materials and criterion testing for measurement of educational outcomes.

256. Weisgerber, R. A., ed. Perspectives in Individualized Learning. F. E. Peacock Publishers, Inc., 1971.
Brings together readings which analyze selected factors underlying the process of individualized learning. The

Learning Theory

experts represented are from the areas of learning theory, individual differences, measurement and evaluation, educational objectives, teacher roles, learning activities, facilities, technology and computer systems. Chapter topics include: underlying assumptions concerning the need for individualized learning; mental abilities as a possible basis for individualized learning; the impact of individual differences on reading; the measurement and accommodation of individual differences; educational objectives; evaluation; the changing role of the teacher; individualized and interactive learning activities; the instructional environment, and computer-assisted instruction.

Chapter 14

MEDIA RESEARCH

The Winter 1974 issue of School Media Quarterly introduced, in its Current Research column, a listing of "School Media Dissertations in Progress." The idea for this came from the Journal of Education for Librarianship, which lists "Doctoral Dissertations Topics Accepted in Library and Information Science." The editors of School Media Quarterly hope to develop a listing of school media dissertations which will tap non-library/information science programs and isolate the school media dissertations found in the JEL list. This current-awareness listing of dissertations on the school library media program is a step toward creating more interest in media research.

Much more research in educational media and technology is needed to define and implement solutions to the needs in education today. In research, media is defined broadly as including all print and non-print aids to instruction. Research is needed, in both education and librarianship, on educational media and technology, its uses, preparation, selection, distribution, research, preservice and in-service education, design and evaluation.

A broad definition of educational research appears in Carter V. Good's Dictionary of Education (2d ed., McGraw-Hill, 1959): "study and investigation in the field of education or bearing upon educational problems." A more specific one is: "an inquiry-oriented activity employing an objective, empirical and controlled methodology, the findings of which must be replicable when subjected to scrutiny by other investigators, must instill a high level of confidence and must be generalizable beyond the local setting in which they are obtained" (Stowe, Richard A., "Research and the Systems Approach as Methodologies for Education," AV Communication Review, Summer, 1973).

The systems approach is a methodology which shows promise in research in new classes of education endeavors. Systems technology has strengthened educational research, and research can make a contribution in educational systems engineering: the two, in a sense, are complementary. The systems approach as research methodology denotes a collection of procedures directed toward realistic effects. Systems methodology may enable the researcher to focus on larger phenomena and hence produce findings of broad significance. The value of a research study or a systems design, however, depends always upon the researcher's ability to abstract effectively from the "rich complexity of reality" (W. T. Morris, The Analysis of Management Decisions. Richard D. Irwin, Inc., 1964.) In general, one might say that research emphasizes the general principle, while systems methodology is generally applied to specific situations.

B. H. Banathy (Instructional Systems, Fearon, 1968) writes: "One of the most conspicuous characteristics of the systems approach is the necessity to change in order to improve the system. It is this characteristic and the feedback structure of the systems design that indicates that the systems approach has an inherent potential which, if properly explored, may offer a framework and a set of strategies for educational innovation and research."

Jerome S. Bruner, writing on The Process of Education (Harvard University Press, 1966), following a conference on new educational methods as early as 1959, says much about the need for research to improve teaching and learning.

Perhaps the best source for keeping abreast of current pertinent research in the field of educational media and technology is the quarterly publication of the Association for Educational Communications and Technology, AV Communication Review, available by subscription or through AECT membership. Audiovisual Instruction, AECT's monthly publication, is another source for current literature in the field of educational technology.

Another important publication is produced by the ERIC Clearinghouse on Media and Technology, Stanford Center for Research and Development in Teaching (School of Education, Stanford University, Stanford, Calif. 94305): the Current Index to Journals in Education (CIJE), a companion publication to Research in Education, also published by ERIC. ERIC also commissions and publishes articles as Occasional Papers. Any material related to education may be sent to this Clearinghouse, though it may be transferred to a more appropriate clearinghouse. The Clearinghouse is most interested in articles and research on television, radio, computers, computer-assisted instruction, films, tapes, filmstrips and slides, individualized instruction, videotape recording, programed instruction, simulation and gaming, and miscellaneous audiovisual aids.

Organizations such as the following have given impetus

to the development of large-scale individualized learning systems:

1. American Institutes for Research, Palo Alto, the developers of the Program for Learning in Accordance with Needs (PLAN), which spans grades 1-12 in language arts, science, social studies and math, and which is marketed by Westinghouse Learning Corp., Palo Alto.

2. The Learning Research and Development Center, Pittsburgh, the developers of Individually Prescribed Instruction (IPI), which spans the elementary grades in language arts and math, with other levels and content areas being developed; presently disseminated by Research for Better Schools, Philadelphia.

3. The Institute for Development of Educational Activities (IDEA) Los Angeles, and the Wisconsin Research and Development Center, Madison, developers of nongraded Individually Guided Education (IGE) which is being disseminated widely in the elementary grades.

4. Center for Individualized Instructional Systems, Durham, developers of Individualized Mathematics Systems (IMS), spanning the elementary grades; widely disseminated in the South.

257. Bloom, Benjamin S., ed. Taxonomy of Educational Objectives, Handbook I: Cognitive Domain. Longmans, Green, 1956.
This earlier publication is included here as writers or students of media research will find it a helpful source of examples of clearly stated objectives and of test and evaluation items appropriate to given objectives.

258. Briggs, L. J., P. L. Campeau, R. M. Gagné, and M. A. May. Instructional Media: A Procedure for the Design of Multi-Media Instruction, A Critical

Review of Research and Suggestions for Future Research. American Institute for Research, 1967.

The selective review of literature on audio-visual media of instruction which is a part of this book includes pertinent and concise information on television, motion pictures, programed instruction and other media. Suggestions are given for future research. In addition, a procedure for choosing media for instruction and examples of use are given. It is a fine overview of the media field.

259. Campbell, Donald T. and Stanley, Julian C. "Experimental and Quasi-Experimental Designs for Research." In Gage N., ed., Handbook of Research on Teaching. Rand McNally, 1963.

Points to the gradual development of design from simple to complex, with explication of the sources of invalidity. Three charts are included which present a clear picture for the researcher of the inherent difficulties in the research plan. The chapter is a fine starting point for the researcher in educational media.

260. Carpenter, C. R. Instructional Film Research Reports. Vol. I. NAVEXOS, P-1220, Technical Report No. SDC 269-7-36. Special Devices Center, 1953.

An early compilation of research reports prepared at Pennsylvania State College with joint sponsorship of the Departments of Army and Navy. The research investigates how to promote use of films and how to increase their effectiveness as an instructional device.

261. Carpenter, C. R. Instructional Film Research Reports. Vol. II NAVEXOS P-1543, Technical Report No. SDC 269-7-61. Special Devices Center, 1956.

Brings up-to-date the earlier volume (see previous entry). Contains outlines of forms used and statistical tables.

262. Culbertson, J. A. and Heneley, S. P., eds. Educational Research: New Perspectives. Interstate, 1963.

Brings together writings of specialists on various areas of educational research, including environment, concepts, methods and training. Two excellent chapters are those by Guba, "Guidelines for the Writing of Proposals," and by Smith, "Critique of Proposals..."

263. Danielson, Wayne A. A Computerized Bibliography of Mass Media Communication Research, 1944-1964.

Magazine Publishers Association, 1967.
A key-word-in-context index and bibliography on mass communications research as reported in social science periodical literature.

264. De Cecco, John P. Educational Technology. Holt, Rinehart, 1964.
These readings bring together research reports and theoretical discussions of psychologists and educators who have contributed to the field of educational technology, programed learning and the psychology of learning. Questions are raised suitable for research on much of the media field.

265. Dreyfus, Les S. Closing the Gap--Research and Practice. University of Wisconsin, 1966.
Examples of significant findings from research studies of media are cited--examples that have been overlooked or ignored by producers of instructional television, for instance. Causes for these gaps between research and practice are discussed and certain solutions are offered. The author urges that all presently available research findings be made accessible to everyone involved in instructional television.

266. Edling, Jack. A Basic Reference Shelf on Instructional Media Research. Using Education Media: Guides to the Literature, Series 1. Stanford University, Institute for Communications Research, 1967.
This annotated bibliography identifies a basic library for the person desiring to interpret, conduct or direct research on educational media.

267. Edwards, Allen L. Techniques of Attitude Scale Construction. Appleton-Century-Crofts, 1957.
The book is not an exhaustive one of psychological scaling methods, but discusses methods that make use of judgments only, responses only, or combinations of the two. Examples are provided.

268. Gage, N. L., ed. Handbook of Research on Teaching. Rand McNally, 1963.
A fine handbook on research in teaching. It summarizes, critically analyzes and integrates many studies on instruction and the media of instruction.

269. Gagné, Robert M. The Conditions of Learning. Holt, Rinehart and Winston, 1965.

Included here because of the particular value of the chapter on resources for learning, this book is a valuable one for the researcher. Different ways of instruction, including the use of media, are discussed.

270. Glaser, Robert, ed. Training Research and Education. John Wiley and Sons, 1965.
Chapters were prepared by experts in various areas of training, and the editor has written a chapter integrating the materials. The book examines training research completed by experimental psychologists and considers its implications for education in general.

271. Good, C. V. Introduction to Educational Research. Appleton-Century-Crofts, 1963.
A good book for the beginning researcher, containing sections on the development of research problems and guides to research literature. Useful in proposal and report writing.

272. Harrison, J. A., ed. European Research in Audio-Visual Aids. Part II: Abstracts. London: National Committee for Audio-Visual Aids in Education, 1966.

273. Hilgard, Ernest R. Theories of Learning. 2nd edition. Appleton-Century-Crofts, 1956.
Discusses the theories of psychologists which are most widely known in educational literature, with experiments to which each theory gives rise. More current theories are also discussed in later chapters.

274. Hoban, Charles F., Jr., and van Ormer, Edward B. Instructional Film Research, 1918-1950. NAVEXOS P-977, Technical Report No. SDC 269-7-19. Special Devices Center, 1950.
This report brings together the results of many widely scattered investigations made over a period of thirty years in the area of training through motion pictures. The report emphasizes four factors: 1) the end-purpose, or objective, for which the film is produced and used; 2) the characteristics of the audience; 3) the content and structure of the film itself; and 4) the context in which the film is presented to the audience.

275. Institute for Communication Research. Educational Television, The Next Ten Years. Stanford University, 1962.

This report of a study commissioned by the Educational Media Branch of the United States Office of Education takes a broad look at completed research. The chapter by Schramm lists 99 references and summarizes many studies on television.

276. Krathwohl, David R., Benjamin S. Bloom, and Bertram B. Masia. Taxonomy of Educational Objectives, Handbook II: Affective Domain. David McKay Co., 1964.

Divided into two parts, this handbook describes the nature of the affective domain and the classification structure prepared for it, as well as describing the classification in detail in Part II and the evaluation of affective objectives at each level of the structure. The Appendices condense Affective Domain and the Cognitive Domain from Handbook I.

277. Lange, Phil C., ed. Programmed Instruction. NSSE, 66th Yearbook, Part II. University of Chicago Press, 1967.

Needed research is identified as well as advantages and limitations of alternative lines of action. Mainly a discussion of principles and theories of programed instruction, but includes other media as well.

278. Lindquist, E. F., ed. Educational Measurement. American Council on Education, 1950.

Remains the best overall treatment of the subject of educational measurement, emphasizing particularly educational achievement.

279. Mager, Robert F. Preparing Objectives for Programmed Instruction. Fearon Publishers, 1962.

If the author's objectives are realized, the reader will complete this self-instructional program in two hours and will be able to identify objectives stated in performance terms, to identify the portion of an objective that describes minimum acceptable performance, and to select test items appropriate to given objectives. These skills are useful in identifying and stating a significant research question.

280. Milkman, Robert L. Entering Audiovisual Competencies, Areas of Graduate Study in Audiovisual Education and Placement Expectations of Master's Degree Candidates in AV Education. A summary report on the Professional AV Education Study (PAVE). New York State Education Department Division of Higher

Education, 1969.
Data from master's degree candidates and recipients in audiovisual education, and from their employers and prospective employers, is gathered and analyzed. Recommendations are made to increase and improve manpower development efforts by the educational media industry, universities and professional organizations.

281. Reid, J. Christopher, and Donald W. MacLennan. Research In Instructional Television and Film. With an introduction by Leslie P. Greenhill. U.S. Office of Education, 1967.
This volume updates the earlier Hoban and van Ormer bibliography (entry no. 274). It contains 333 detailed abstracts of research studies and has a topical index.

282. Salomon, G. What Does It Do to Johnny? A Cognitive-Functionalistic View of Research in Media, 1969. ERIC Document, 1969.
Research in media needs to relate itself to research in other fields. Thus it needs to deal with function of stimuli, laying the foundation for a prescriptive theory that concerns itself with the relationship between how things are presented and how they are learned.

283. Siegel, S. Nonparametric Statistics for the Behavioral Sciences. McGraw, 1956.
A comprehensive collection of nonparametric statistical tools; behavioral science researchers will find useful the well-described procedures and excellent examples.

284. Tobias, Sigmund. Dimensions of Teachers' Attitudes toward Instructional Media. ERIC Document Service, Bethesda, Md., 1967.
Factor analysis of the 179 ratings yielded three factors: 1) programed instruction; 2) traditional teaching aids; and 3) audio-visual devices. Teachers have significantly less favorable attitudes toward terms which directly connote automation than toward comparable terms that are not identified with automation.

285. Trow, William C. Teacher and Technology: New Design for Learning. Appleton-Century-Crofts, 1963.
A study of "the relation between the means available for instruction and their effectiveness in the different kinds of learning experiences that are provided." Reviews the historical development of instructional media as a

background to the presentation of new concepts in teaching technology.

286. Wagner, Robert W. <u>A Series of Motion Picture Documents of Communication Theory and the New Educational Media.</u> Ohio State University, 1966.

A series of 40 films was developed for college-level instruction in aspects of communication theory and the educational media. The topics covered are: 1) the information explosion; 2) process of communication; and 3) the teacher of technology. The report is intended to stimulate thinking on how to teach with motion pictures.

Chapter 15

ASPECTS OF CHANGE

All the changes in educational media and educational technology dictate an evaluation of the whole teaching and learning process as it exists in our schools and colleges today. We are perhaps previewing a revolution in education which is still years ahead. New educational media, new technology, new evaluation methods, changes in behavioral objectives, new ways to motivate the student--all will have an effect, but it is instructional management that will change the future of education.

Alvin Toffler, author of Future Shock (Random House, 1970), first set forth his ideas on education in that book. In Learning for Tomorrow (Random House, 1974) he elaborates on many of these ideas. He writes of an approach to learning and to curriculum which has the goals of helping students cope with the future and participate in the community, and of changing the values of society.

The future of educational technology was surveyed at the 1973 Educational Media Leadership Conference meeting at Lake Okoboji in Iowa. (For the last eighteen years the conference has been sponsored by the University of Iowa and AECT.) Specific aspects of the future of instructional technology were: The Future of Society, 2002 A.D.; The Future Education and Curriculum Trends; Future Strategies for

Aspects of Change

Improving Instructional Technology; the Future Management and Funding of Media Programs; Instructional Technologies; A Concept for A. D. 2000; Change Processes: An Exploration into Strategies Moving Into the Future; and The Future of Instructional Technology: A Mediated Package.

An introductory article in Audiovisual Instruction, January, 1974, details the concerns as the NCATE-Accredited Teacher Education Programs are considered and as AECT views the future of teacher education. It is important as we consider aspects of change to note these goals or guidelines, which include:

> The study of teaching and learning theory includes a basic understanding of all modern media and technology and of the process of communications, as related to learning and the instructional task. The systematic use of newer media and technology should be a part of the teacher trainee's experience as he approaches the study of teaching and learning theory. Newer media and technology can particularly serve the clinical needs of the Professional Study Component of modern teacher education programs. And lastly, research and development in the area of newer media and technology should be reflected in the teacher education program. (From Basic Guidelines for Media and Technology in Teacher Education, AECT, 1971.)

Edgar Dale, in "Toward Excellence in Instruction" (Audiovisual Instruction, September, 1973), says: "to meet the instructional needs of learners requires universal access to the excellence that 'the best and wisest parent's wants for his own child' [quoting from John Dewey]. I mean excellent instructional materials, excellent teachers, cooperative parents, rich, challenging experiences both in and out of school."

287. Brown, James W. and James W. Thornton. New Media in Higher Education. Association for Higher Education and the Division of Audiovisual Instructional Service, NEA, 1963.
The premise of this earlier book is that potential solutions to the problems now confronting higher education will be found within the fields of new media. There are chapters on administration and on instructional aims and new media--both areas which need further exploration in higher education. The book is the result of work of a committee of the Department of Audio-Visual Instruction, working with heads of audiovisual centers.

288. Eurich, Alvin C. High School 1980: the Shape of the Future in American Secondary Education. Pitman, 1970.
Discussion by 24 educators on the future of secondary education in 1980, and the changes brought about by social, technological and cultural changes in the nation. John W. Longhary, writing on teaching technology, presents an interesting and unique approach, stressing utilization of a world-wide instructional television system to make the world more cognizant of a world society. His emphasis is on independent learning, with the teacher of the future seen as an instructional manager.

289. Ferkiss, Victor C. Technological Man. Mentor, 1969.
Reflects the thinking of prophets such as McLuhan, Koestler, Kahn and others. The author presents a picture of the technological past, present and future. Excellent bibliography, as well as a section of notes. A thought-provoking book.

290. Footlick, Jerrold K. Education--a New Era. Newsbook, National Observer, 1966.
The new learning--abandonment of many traditional concepts of learning; the new revolution--new math, new sciences; teaching--the new profession.

291. Harrison, J. A., ed. European Research in Audio-Visual Aids, Part I, Bibliography. Strasbourg, Austria, Council of Europe, 1966.
Published in two documents, bibliography and abstracts. The bibliographic section includes academic research, experiments; the abstracts section includes only authoritative research. Well-organized bibliography.

292. Jordan, Robert T. Tomorrow's Library: Direct Access and Delivery. Bowker, 1970.
Concerned with experiments in home delivery or mail service to users of the library; also contains interesting historical background on early libraries. It is primarily a report of a conference on "Books by Mail, "San Francisco, June, 1967. Proposals include a book catalog, universal library cards, speedier and more efficient access.

293. Lifton, Walter M., ed. Educating For Tomorrow: the Role of Media, Career Development and Society. Wiley, 1970.
Written to help schools, colleges and industry use educational media to effectuate pupil values and goals and to transmit the culture. Worthwhile for large specialized collections in educational methods.

294. Loughary, John W. Man-Machine Systems in Education. Harper, 1966.
Co-authors are John F. Cogswell, Jack V. Edling, Frank Farmer, Alvin Grossman, Robert L. Rowe and Murray Tondow. Media technology and the learning process, as well as new media applications are among the emphases of this book. For the future, the preparation of educators in usage of computers and new media is an important consideration. Describes probable future developments of man-machine systems in education.

295. McLuhan, Marshall, and Quentin Fiore. The Medium Is the Massage. Bantam Books, 1967.
"The technology of our times is reshaping and restructuring patterns of social interdependence and every aspect of our personal life." Societies have always been shaped more by the nature of media than by content of media. It is a programed text in itself, in a way. Visual media, the environment that man creates, all become his media by defining his role.

296. McLuhan, Marshall. Understanding Media: the Extension of Man. McGraw-Hill, 1964.
A description of the totally new environment that has been created in the electronic age. The new era, the new age of education is programed for discovery rather than instruction.

297. McLuhan, Marshall. Verbi-Voco-Visual Explorations. Something Else Press, 1967.

A brief scanning of this book will give the reader the meaning of the word "media." Originally issued as No. 8 of Explorations, a periodical.

298. Meetham, Roger. Information Retrieval: The Essential Technology. Doubleday, 1970.

The essential function of the library in today's world of technology is discussed in detail. The most pertinent chapters are on the Library as a System, and Classification and Description. Fact retrieval from any data base is discussed in the final chapter. The book is well-illustrated, attractive, and of interest to librarians, teachers or anyone interested in new ideas in education.

299. Miller, Richard I. Perspectives on Educational Change. Appleton-Century-Crofts, 1967.

The process of change--not the direction of change or its evaluation--is the principal emphasis of this book. The author states that "hopefully, books of this general nature will be rendered obsolete in a few years by the rapid advancement in specific dimensions of the important areas." This collection includes articles by J. Lloyd Trump, Harold Wigren, William Alexander and Henry Brickell. An excellent chapter is "The Role of Local School Systems in Change," by Henry M. Brickell. Richard A. Gibboney writes on "The Role of the State Education Department in Educational Change."

300. National School Public Relations Association. Technology in Education: Education U.S.A. Special Report; New Developments in Technology Herald an Impending Revolution in American Education. National School Public Relations Association, 1967.

The editors of Education U.S.A. considered that the implications of the impending technological revolution in education, with its substantial financial investment and potential for upsetting the status quo, required a special report. This concise collection of what many leaders in education and industry are thinking and saying about the effects of technology on learning and education emphasizes particularly the role of the computer in education.

301. Niemi, John A. Mass Media and Adult Education. Educational Technology Publications, 1971.

Collected papers which describe important developments in the use of the mass media in adult education. Traces the history of educational television in the United

States and concludes that educators are lacking in imagination in the whole approach to education. Constructive criticism.

302. Platt, John R. Perception and Change: Projections for Survival. University of Michigan Press, 1970.
Collection of essays discussing current changes in the world, and particularly in education. The author stresses the diversity in education, where there is the greatest need for diversity. A perceptive book.

303. Postlethwait, S. N., J. Novak and H. T. Murray, Jr. The Audio-Tutorial Approach to Learning. Burgess, 1969.
This revised version is an important contribution for its explanation of the audio-tutorial process, the model for media-based self-instruction in numerous subject matters, grade levels and institutions.

304. Rossi, Peter H. The New Media and Education: Their Impact on Society, edited by Peter H. Rossi and Bruce J. Biddle. National Opinion Research Center, Monographs in Social Research. Aldine, 1966.
A collection of essays speculating on the roles that may be played in the next decade in American society by the new educational media. Sections include: an overview, the concept of an educational medium and types of media, the adoption of media in education, media's impact on education and the impact of educational media and education on Western society.

305. Rossoff, Martin. The School Library and Educational Change. Library Science Text Series. Libraries Unlimited, 1971.
This small book is an excellent background for understanding the school library media center and its operation. It is not a handbook. It is of value to the teacher as well and would be a good addition to the professional library, which subject is covered in one chapter of the book. The purpose of the author is to define the place of the school library in contemporary education--what it is, where it came from, where it is going, what it contains and how it is organized. Most important of all, the author points out the place of the library media center in the pattern of classroom instruction today.

306. Rostow, Eugene V. President's Task Force on Communications Policy. Final Report. U.S. Government Printing Office, 1968.

Recommends strengthened federal powers to form public policy in telecommunication. Monopoly of telecommunication should remain the exception, not the rule, so as to produce maximal consumer satisfaction and technological advancement.

307. Smith, Karl U. Cybernetic Principles of Learning and Educational Design, by Karl U. Smith and Margaret Foltz Smith. Holt, 1966.

A new scientific approach to human learning phenomena. The theme of the book is that the cybernetics interpretation of behavior represents not a specialized field of interest but a general theory of behavior organization which challenges conventional theories. The learning situation must be designed to fit the control capabilities of the learner.

308. Thornton, James W. New Media and College Teaching, ed. by James W. Thornton, Jr., and James W. Brown. Department of Audiovisual Instruction, Association for Higher Education, National Education Association, 1968.

Since the publication of New Media and Higher Education five years previously, the most obvious changes have been in new relationships between men and machines.

309. Tyler, I. Keith and Catherine M. Williams. Educacational Communication in a Revolutionary Age, edited by I. Keith Tyler and Catherine M. Williams. Charles A. Jones, 1973.

Collection of papers by outstanding authorities, commemorating the retirement of Edgar Dale from Ohio State University. The collection has two major themes-- education is changing, and needs for the future center around individual needs of students. Dale calls for creative reactions to communications experiences and for instruments of evaluation.

310. Van Hoffman, Nicholas. The Multiuniversity: A Personal Report On What Happens to Today's Students at American Universities. Holt, 1966.

Firsthand report on what one university is like to the people who live in it. Reactions of students, feelings of anonymity, etc.

Chapter 16

SELECT BIBLIOGRAPHY OF PERIODICALS ON EDUCATIONAL MEDIA

This bibliography of some one hundred periodicals was formulated from these basic sources of information:

1. The University of Colorado, Norlin Library and branch libraries' current periodicals sections.

2. The University of Kansas, Watson Library current periodicals section.

3. The Kansas State University, Farrell Library current periodicals section.

4. The Wichita State University, Ablah Library current periodicals section.

5. Emporia Kansas State College, William Allen White Library current periodicals section.

6. The periodicals collection of Wichita Public Library.

The bibliography is arranged in broad subject categories, and each entry includes: title of periodical, frequency of publication, place of publication and price.

EDUCATIONAL DATA PROCESSING (EDP) AND COMPUTER TECHNOLOGY

Communications of the ACM (Association for Computing Machinery)**

**Publications also containing some technical articles.

Monthly, membership (non-members, $15.00) Editor, C. C. Gotlieb, 211 East 43rd Street, New York, New York 10017.

The Computer Bulletin**
Quarterly, $2.80. Editor, M. Bridger. British Computer Society, 23 Dorset Square, London, N.W. 1, England.

Computer Digest
Monthly, $9.00. Editor, Edith H. Goodman, American Data Processing, Inc., Book Building, Detroit, Michigan 48226.

Computer World: newsweekly for the computer community.
Weekly, $9.00. Editor, Alan Taylor, Computerworld, Inc., 60 Austin Street, Newton, Massachusetts 02160.

Computers and Automation**
Monthly, $15.00. Editor, Edmund C. Berkeley, Berkeley Enterprises, Inc., 815 Washington Street, Newtonville 60, Massachusetts 02160.

Computers and the Humanities
5/yr. $7.50. Editor, Prof. Joseph Raben, English Department, Queens College, Flushing, New York 11367.

Computing Reviews* **
Bi-monthly, $15.00. Editor, Ed. A. Finerman, Assn. for Computing Machinery, 211 East 43rd Street, New York, New York 10017.

Datamation**
Monthly, free to qualified personnel; others, $15.00. Editor, Robert B. Frost, F. D. Thompson Publications, Inc., 1830 W. Olympic Blvd., Los Angeles, Calif. 90006.

Data Processing Digest* **
Monthly, $24.00. Editor, Margaret Milligan, Data Processing Digest, Inc., 1140 S. Robertson Blvd., Los Angeles, Calif. 90035.

Data Processing for Education
Monthly, $24.00. Editor, Dr. John W. Sullivan, American Data Processing, Inc., Book Tower, Detroit, Michigan 48226.

*Information Indexes.

Bibliography of Periodicals 115

Data Processing Magazine: Incorporating Data Processing for Management and Data Processing for Science Engineering.
  Monthly, $8.50. Editor, Edith H. Goodman, North American Publishing Company, 134 N. 13th Street, Philadelphia, Pa.

Data Processor
  Monthly, $6.00. International Business Machines Corp., 112 East Post Road, White Plains, New York.

DPMA Quarterly
  Quarterly, $5.00. Editor, R. Calvin Elliott, Data Processing Management Association, 505 Busse Highway, Park Ridge, Ill. 60068.

EDUCOM (Bulletin of the Interuniversity Communications Council)
  Six issues a year, $10.00. Editor, Hilda Jones, IUCC, 36th floor, 4200 Fifth Avenue, Pittsburgh, Pa. 15213.

IBM Computing Report (IBM Journal of Research and Development)
  Quarterly, $5.00. Editor, D. T. Sanders, International Business Machines Corp., Data Processing Division, 112 East Post Road, White Plains, New York 10601.

I.E.E.E. Transactions on Human Factors in Electronics**
  Frequency varies, $17.00. Institute of Electrical and Electronic Engineers, Inc., Box A, Lenox Hill Station, New York, New York 10021.

Information and Records Management
  Bi-monthly, price not given. Editor, Rodd Exelbert, Information and Records Management, Inc., 257 Park Avenue, New York, New York 10010.

Journal of Computer and Systems Sciences
  Quarterly, $20.00. Editorial Board, Academic Press, 111 Fifth Avenue, New York, New York 10003.

Journal of Data Management (Data Processing Management Assn.)
  Monthly, $5.00. Editor, Jack Linden. 524 Busse Highway, Park Ridge, Ill. 60068.

TELEVISION AND RADIO COMMUNICATIONS

1. GENERAL READING

EBU Review, Part B.
Bi-monthly, $5.00. European Broadcasting Union Administrative Office, 1 rue de Varembe, Geneva, Switzerland. (Part A, bi-monthly, technical, $3.50.)

Educational Broadcasting International
Quarterly, $6.50. Editor, F. Marriott, Wynn Williams Publishers, Ltd., Centenary Bldgs., King Street, Wrexham, England, and Headington Hill Hall, Oxford OX3 OBW, England.

Educational Broadcasting Review (supersedes NAEB Journal, National Association of Educational Broadcasters)
Bi-monthly, $6.00. Editor, Allen E. Koenig, Ohio State University, 3 Lord Hall, Columbus, Ohio 43210. (Available from NAEB, 1346 Connecticut Avenue, N.W., Washington, D.C. 20036).

Educational Broadcasting; The International Journal of Audio and Visual Learning
Bi-monthly, $20.00. Editors, Hal Spector and Martin H. Naldman, Acolyte Publications, Inc., 825 S. Barrington Ave., Los Angeles, Calif. 90049.

Educational Television
Monthly, $8.00. C. S. Tepfer Publishing Company, Inc., 607 Main Street, Ridgefield, Conn. 06877.

Educational Television Newsletter (ETV Newsletter)
Fortnightly, $4.00. Editor, C. S. Tepfer, ETV Newsletter Co., 10 Poplar Road, Ridgefield, Conn. 06877.

Educational Television International
Quarterly, $10.00 (Individuals), $15.00 (Institutions) Pergamon Press, Inc., Maxwell, House, Fairview Park, Elmsford, New York 10523.

Journal of Broadcasting
Quarterly, $6.00. Editor, Jr. John M. Kitteoss, Association for Professional Broadcasting Education, University of Southern California, Los Angeles, Calif. 90007.

Television
Monthly, $6.00. Société des Editions Radio, 42 rue

Bibliography of Periodicals

Jacob, Paris (6e), France.

Television Quarterly (National Academy of Television Arts and Sciences)
4 times a year, $5.00. Editor, William Bluem, 54 W. 40th Street, New York, New York 10018.

2. TECHNICAL PUBLICATIONS

Broadcasting
Weekly, $8.50; with yearbook in January, $13.50. Editor, Sol Taishoff, Broadcasting Publications, Inc., 1735 DeSales, N.W., Washington, D.C. 20036.

Electronics
Fortnightly, $6.00. Editor, Lewis H. Young, McGraw-Hill, 330 W. 42nd Street, New York, New York 10036.

Electronics World
Monthly, $5.00. Editor, William Stocklin, Ziff-Davis Publishing Co., 1 Park Avenue, New York, New York 10016.

IBM Journal of Research and Development
Quarterly, $5.00. Editor, Al L. Samuel. International Business Machines Corp., 590 Madison Avenue, New York, New York 10010.

I.E.E.E. Transactions on Broadcast and Television Receivers
Frequency varies, $17.00. Institute of Electrical and Electronics Engineers, Inc., Box A, Lenox Hill Station, New York 10021.

I.E.E.E. Transactions on Broadcasting
Frequency varies, $17.00, Institute of Electrical and Electronics Engineers, Inc., Box A, Lenox Hill Station, New York 10021.

NRI Journal (National Radio Institute)
Bi-monthly, $2.00. Editor, William F. Dunn, National Radio Institute, 3939 Wisconsin Avenue, Washington, D.C. 20016.

RCA Review
Quarterly, $2.00. Editor, C. C. Foster, RCA Laboratories, Princeton, New Jersey.

PROGRAMED INSTRUCTION

Journal of Programed Instruction
   Quarterly, $7.50. Editor, Lincoln F. Hanson, 453 Strawtown Road, West Nyack, New York.

NSPI Journal (National Society for Programmed Instruction); supersedes Programed Instruction)
   10 times a year, membership $5.00, non-members $20.00. Editor, Jack Weppner, National Society for Programmed Instruction, Trinity University, 715 Stadium Drive, San Antonio, Texas 78212.

Programmed Learning and Educational Technology
   Quarterly, £3 (postage 3s); single copy, 17s 6d; Sweet and Maxwell, Ltd., 11 New Fetter Lane, London, E.C.4, England.

MICRO PHOTO INFORMATION PROCESSING

The Micro Photo Reader: National Newsletter of Microfilming for Libraries.
   Quarterly, free. Editor, Jean S. Reid, Bell & Howell, Inc., Micro-Photo Division, 701 Shaw Avenue, Cleveland, Ohio 44112.

Microcosm
   6 times a year, free circulation. University Microfilms, Inc., Library Services, Xerox Corp., 300 N. Zeeb Road, Ann Arbor, Michigan 48106.

National Micro News
   Six times a year, $7.50. Editor, Vernon D. Tate, National Microfilm Association, Box 386, Annapolis, Maryland 21401.

Photo Methods for Industry (PMI)
   Gellert Publishing Corporation, 33 W. 60th Street, New York, New York 10023.

EQUIPMENT AND MATERIALS

Audio
   Monthly, $5.00. North American Publishing Co., 134 No. Thirteenth Street, Philadelphia, Pa. 19107.

Bibliography of Periodicals 119

The Audio Visual Equipment Directory (A Guide to Current Models of Audio Visual Equipment)
    Annual, $6.00. National AudioVisual Association, 3150 Spring Street, Fairfax, Virginia 22030.

Blue Book of Audio-Visual Materials
    Annual, $1.00 (Included with subscription to AV Guide: The Learning Media Magazine). Educational Screen and AudioVisual Guide, 423 S. Wabash, Chicago, Ill. 60605.

Educational Electronic Equipment and Buyers Guide
    Irregular, no price. Milton Publishing Company, Ltd., 31 Percy Street, London, England.

Educational Equipment and Materials
    Quarterly, $2.00. Editor, Edwin M. Perrin, Robinson-Phillips, Inc., 60 East 42nd Street, New York, New York 10017.

EPIE Forum (Educational Productions Information Exchange)
    Monthly, 9/year, $25.00. Editor, P. Kenneth Komoski, EPIE Institute, 527 Lexington Avenue, New York, New York 10017.

P/I (Product Information) for Schools
    Bi-monthly, $3.00. Editor, Paul Abramson, Management Publishing Group, School Management Magazine Publishing Company, 22 W. Putnam Avenue, Greenwich, Conn. 06830.

Previews
    Monthly, $5.00. Editor, Phyllis Levy, R. R. Bowker Co., 1180 Avenue of Americas, New York, New York 10036.

School Management
    Monthly, $8.00. Editor, Paul Abramson, 22 Putnam, Greenwich, Conn. 06830.

School Product News
    Monthly, free. Editor, J. Arlen Marsh. Industrial Publishing Company, 812 Huron Road, Cleveland, Ohio 44115.

School Progress
    Monthly, $5.00. Editor, Harry F. Coles, 57 Bloor Street, W. Toronto, 5, Canada.

GENERAL INFORMATION PERIODICALS

These include trends and implications for the field of educational media and technology, including the state of the art, information concerning innovations and developments in all areas of educational media and technology.

Audio-Visual Communications (formerly Film Audio-Visual Communications)
    Bi-monthly, $3.00. United Business Publications, 200 Madison Avenue, New York, New York 10016.

Audiovisual Instruction
    10 issues a year, $12.00 (included with membership in Association for Educational Communications and Technology). Howard B. Hitchens, Jr., Editor. Association for Educational Communications and Technology, 1201 Sixteenth Street, N.W., Washington, D.C. 20036.

Automated Education Letter
    Monthly, $18.00. Editor, Edith H. Goodman, Automated Education Center, Box 2658, Detroit, Michigan 48231.

AV Communication Review
    Quarterly, $13.00 (included with membership in Association for Educational Communications and Technology). Howard B. Hitchens, Jr., editor. Association for Educational Communications and Technology, 1201 Sixteenth Street, N.W., Washington, D.C. 20036.

AV Guide; The Learning Media Magazine
    Monthly, $4.00; Blue Book in August, $1.00. Editor, Henry C. Ruark, Educational Screen and Audiovisual Guide, 434 South Wabash, Chicago, Ill. 60605.

The Booklist
    Bi-monthly, $12.00. American Library Association, 50 E. Huron Street, Chicago, Ill. 60611.

Educational Media
    Monthly, $10.00. 1015 Florence Street, Fort Worth, Texas 76102.

Educational Media International
    Quarterly, no cost given. Editor, Peter J. Vernon, Modino Press, Ltd., 68 Queen Street, London, Ec4N, England.

Bibliography of Periodicals   121

Educational Resources and Techniques
    Quarterly, $2.00. Texas Association of Educational Technology, P. O. Drawer W, University Station, Austin, Texas 78712.

Educational Technology
    Monthly, $18.00. 140 Sylvan Avenue, Englewood Cliffs, New Jersey 07632.

Journal of Broadcasting
    Quarterly, $6.00. Editor, John M. Kittross, Association for Professional Broadcasting Education, University of Southern California, University Park, Los Angeles, Calif. 90007.

Journal of Educational Technology
    3 issues a year, $10.00. Editor, Norman MacKenzie, Councils and Education Press, Ltd., 10 Queen Anne Street, London, W1M9LD, England.

Media and Methods
    Monthly (September-May), $5.00. Media & Methods Institute, Inc., 314 N. Thirteenth Street, Philadelphia, Pa. 19107.

Modern Media Teacher
    Bi-monthly during the school year (5 issues), $5.00. George A. Pflaum, 33 W. Fifth Street, Dayton, Ohio 45402.

NAEB Journal (National Association of Educational Broadcasters)
    Bi-monthly, $5.00. Editor, Colby Lewis, Gregory Hall, Urbana, Illinois.

NALLD Journal (Newsletter of the National Association of Language Laboratory Directors)
    Quarterly, $6.00 members; $9.00 library rate. Newsletter of the National Association of Language Laboratory Directors, Ohio University, Athens, Ohio 45701.

Phi Delta Kappan
    9 issues a year, $5.00. Editor, Stanley Elam, Phi Delta Kappa, Inc., Eighth Street and Union Avenue, Bloomington, Ind. 47401.

School Library Journal
    Monthly, (September-May), $10.00. R. R. Bowker Co.,

1180 Avenue of the Americas, New York, New York 10036. Published also as a part of Library Journal, midmonth issue.

School Media Quarterly (formerly School Libraries)
Quarterly, membership (single copies may be purchased from the executive secretary for $2.00). American Association of School Libraries, 50 E. Huron Street, Chicago, Ill. 60611.

Stereo Review
Monthly, $6.00. Ziff-Davis Publishing Company, 1 Park Avenue, New York, New York 10016.

Teachers' Guide to Media and Methods
Monthly, $3.00. Editor, Frank McLoughlin, Media and Methods Institute, 134 N. Thirteenth Street, Philadelphia, Pa. 19107.

Television Quarterly
4 times a year, membership, others $5.00. Editor, William Bleum, 54 W. 40th, New York, New York 10018.

Times (London) Educational Supplement
Weekly, $10.00. Editor, Walter James, Times Publishing Company, Ltd., Printing House Square, London E.C.4, England.

Training in Business and Industry
Monthly, $5.00. Editor, Wallace Hanson, Gellert Publishing Company, 33 W. 60th Street, New York, New York 10023.

Training News (Human Relations Training News)
4/year, $2.00. Editor, Cyril R. Mill, National Training Laboratories, 1201 Sixteenth Street, N.E., Washington, D.C. 20036.

Visual Communications Instructor
Monthly, Circulation controlled. Syndicate Magazines, 25 W. 24th Street, New York, New York 10036.

Visual Education
Monthly, $4.00. Editor, Peter Vernon, National Commission for Audio-Visual Aids in Education, 33 Queen Anne Street, London, England.

RESEARCH ORIENTED - TECHNICAL

The periodicals deal with topics such as uses of educational media in the schools, programed instruction, computer-assisted instruction.

American Educational Research Journal
4 times a year, $6.00. Editor, Frederick B. Davis, AERA, 1201 Sixteenth Street, N.W., Washington, D.C. 20036.

Journal of Applied Psychology
Bi-monthly, $10.00. Editor, Kenneth E. Clark, American Psychological Association, 1200 17th Street, N.W., Washington, D.C. 20036.

Journal of Educational Psychology
Bi-monthly, $10.00. Editor, Raymond G. Kuhlen, American Psychological Association, 1200 17th Street, N.W., Washington, D.C. 20036.

Journal of Educational Research
10 times a year, $10.00. Editor, Wilson Thiede, Dembar Educational Research Services, Inc., Box 1605, Madison, Wisconsin 53701.

Journal of Experimental Education
Quarterly, $10.00. Editor, John Schmid, Dembar Educational Research Services, Inc., Box 1605, Madison, Wisconsin 53701.

Journal of Teacher Education
National Commission on Teacher Education and Professional Standards, Quarterly, $8.00. Editor, D. D. Darland, National Educational Association, 1201 Sixteenth Street, N.W., Washington, D.C. 20036.

Research in Education (ERIC)
(Including Current Index to Journals in Education, a new monthly publication, a companion publication to Research in Education)
Monthly, $11.00. Educational Research Information Center, U.S. Department of Health, Education and Welfare, Office of Education, Bureau of Research, Washington, D.C. Subscription to: Superintendent of Documents, U.S. Gov't. Printing Office, Washington, D.C. 20402.

Review of Educational Research
 5 times a year, membership, non-members, $7.50. Editor, Jacob T. Hunt, National Education Association, 1201 Sixteenth Street, N.W., Washington, D.C. 20036.

AUTOMATION OF LIBRARIES

American Documentation
 Quarterly, membership, non-members, $18.50. Editor, Arthur W. Elias, American Documentation Institute, Information Science, 200 P Street, N.W., Washington, D.C. 20036.

American Libraries: Bulletin of the American Library Association.
 Monthly, bi-monthly for July, August, membership. Editor, J. Gordon Burke. American Library Association, 50 E. Huron Street, Chicago, Illinois 60611.

American Library Association Library Technology Project: Library Technology Reports (also Annual Report)
 Bi-monthly, $100. Editor, William P. Cole, Library Technology Project, ALA, 50 E. Huron Street, Chicago, Illinois 60611.

ASIS Newsletter
 Bi-monthly, membership. American Society for Information Science, 2000 P Street N.W., Washington, D.C. 20036.

Bulletin of the Medical Library Association
 4 times a year, $10.00. Editor, Alfred N. Brandon, Mt. Royal and Guilford Avenues, Baltimore 2, Maryland.

College and Research Libraries
 Bi-monthly, membership; non-members, $10.00. Editor, Richard M. Dougherty. Association of College and Research Libraries, ALA, 50 E. Huron Street, Chicago, Illinois 60611.

EDUCOM
 Six issues a year, $10.00. Editor, Hilda Jones, IUCC, 36th Floor, 4200 Fifth Avenue, Pittsburgh, Pa. 15213.

Information Retrieval and Library Automation Letter (formerly Information Retrieval Letter)

Monthly, $24.00. Editor, Lowell H. Hattery, American Data Processing Co., 410 Book Building, Detroit, Mich. 48226.

Information Scientist
3/yr, $3.00. Editor, R. L. Ballard, Institute of Information Scientists, 5-7 Russian Row, London, E.C.2, England.

Journal of Documentation
Quarterly, membership. 3 Belgrave Square, London, England.

Journal of Library Automation
Quarterly, $10.00. Editor, Frederick G. Kilgour, American Library Association, Information Science and Automation Division, 50 East Huron Street, Chicago, Illinois 60611.

Library Journal
Semi-monthly, $15.00. R. R. Bowker, Co., 1180 Avenue of the Americas, New York, New York 10036.

Library Quarterly
Quarterly, $8.00. Editor, Howard Winger, University of Chicago Press, 5750 Ellis Avenue, Chicago, Illinois 60637.

Library Resources and Technical Services
Quarterly, membership; non-members, $8.00. American Library Association, 50 E. Huron Street, Chicago, Illinois 60611.

Library Trends
Quarterly, $8.00. Editor, Herbert Goldhor, University of Illinois Graduate School of Library Science, Urbana, Ill. (Subscriptions Department of University of Illinois Press, Urbana, Illinois 61803).

MEDIA INNOVATIONS

(University, College, Junior College)

American Association of University Professors Bulletin
4 times a year, $3.50. Editor, Warren C. Middleton,

AAUP, 1785 Massachusetts Avenue N.W., Washington, D.C. 20036.

American School and University
Monthly, $8.00. Editor, James E. Talbot. North American Publishing Company, 41 East 42nd St., New York, New York 10017.

AV Guide; The Learning Media Magazine
Monthly, $4.00 (Blue Book in August, $1.00). Editor, Denise A. Wenger, H.S. Gillette, 434 S. Wabash Avenue, Chicago, Illinois 60605.

College and University Bulletin
Fortnightly, October-June, $7.00. Editor, Carol MacGuineas, Association for Higher Education, 1201 Sixteenth Street, N.W., Washington, D.C. 20036.

College Management
Monthly, $6.00. Editor, Paul Abrahamson, Management Publishing Groups, 22 N. Putnam Avenue, Greenwich, Connecticut 06830.

College and University Business
Monthly, $10.00. Editor, Harold W. Herman, McGraw-Hill Publishing Company, 1050 Merchandise Mart, Chicago, Ill. 60654.

Educational Leadership
Monthly, (October-June) $5.50. Editor, Robert R. Leeper, Association for Supervision and Curriculum Development, 1201 Sixteenth Street, N.W., Washington, D.C. 20036.

Educational Record
Quarterly, $6.00. Editor, Edward J. Sholen, Jr., 1785 Massachusetts Avenue, N.W., Washington, D.C. 20036.

EDUCOM (Bulletin of the Interuniversity Communications Council)
Six issues a year, $10.00. Editor, Hilda Jones, IUCC, 36th floor, 4200 Fifth Avenue, Pittsburgh, Pa. 15213.

Journal of Higher Education
Monthly, (Oct.-June) $6.00. Editor, C. Grey Austin, Ohio State University Press, 164 W. 19th Avenue, Columbus, Ohio 43210.

Bibliography of Periodicals 127

Journal of Library Automation
Quarterly, $10.00. Editor, Frederick G. Kilgour, American Library Association, Information Sciences and Automation Division, 50 East Huron Street, Chicago, Ill. 60611.

North Central Association Quarterly
(North Central Association of Colleges and Secondary Schools) Quarterly, $4.00. Editor, Norman Burns, 5454 N. Shore Drive, Chicago, Illinois.

Teachers' College Journal now Contemporary Education
Monthly, (October-June), $7.50. Editor, M. Dale Baughman, Reeves Hall, Terre Haute, Ind. 47800.

Teachers' College Record
Monthly, October-May, $7.50. Editor, Maxine Greene, Columbia University, Teachers' College, 525 W. 120th Street, New York 10027.

INDUSTRIAL AND COMMERCIAL PUBLICATIONS

Electronic Age
Quarterly. Editor, Julea Kaslow, Radio Corp. of America, 30 Rockefeller Plaza, New York, New York 10020.

Electronic Trends
Monthly, $25.00 to members, $100, others. Editor, John S. Hoover, Electronic Industries Association, Marketing-Service Department, 2001 Eye Street, N.W., Washington, D.C. 20036.

Training in Business and Industry
Monthly, $5.00. Editor, Wallace Hanson, Gellert Publishing Company, 33 W. 60th Street, New York, New York 10023.

PMI (Photo Methods for Industry)
Monthly, $5.00. Gellert Publishing Corp., 33 W. 60th Street, New York, New York 10023.

TECHNOLOGY, AUTOMATION, COMMUNICATIONS

AEDS Monitor
Monthly, $15.00. Editor, Dr. Sylvia Charp, Association

for Educational Data Systems, 1201 16th Street, N.W., Washington, D.C. 10036.

Contemporary Psychology
Monthly, $10.00. Editor, Fillmore H. Sanford, American Psychological Association, Inc., 1200 17th Street, Washington, D.C. 20036.

Control Engineering
Monthly, $10.00. Editor, B. K. Ledgerwood. Reuben H. Donnelly Corp., 466 Lexington Ave., New York, New York 10017.

Film Library Quarterly
Quarterly, membership, non-members, $8.00. Film Library Information Council, 17 W. Sixtieth Street, New York, New York 10023.

Film News: The International Review of AV Materials and Equipment.
Bi-monthly, $6.00. Film News Company, 250 W. 57th Street, New York, New York 10019.

I.E.E.E. Transactions on Communication Technology
Frequency varies, $17.00. Institute of Electrical and Electronic Engineer, Inc., Box A, Lenox Hill Station, New York, New York 10021.

I.E.E.E. Transactions on Engineering Writing and Speech
Frequency varies, $17.00. Institute of Electrical and Electronic Engineers, Inc., Box A, Lenox Hill Station, New York, New York 10021.

The Journal of Communication
Quarterly, $5.00. Executive Secretary, Dr. R. Wayne Pall, University of Montana, Missoula, Montana 59801.

Journal of the University Film Association
Quarterly, membership (non-members, $4.00). Robert W. Wagner, Department of Photography and Cinema, Ohio State University, 156 W. Nineteenth Avenue, Columbus, Ohio 43210.

Journal of Verbal Learning and Verbal Behavior
Bi-monthly, $9.50. Editor, Leo Postman, Academic Press, Inc., 111 Fifth Avenue, New York, New York 10003.

Bibliography of Periodicals

Landers Film Reviews
 Monthly, $30.00. Landers Associates, Box 69760, Los Angeles, California 90069.

Preview
 Irregular, apply. NET Film Service and Indiana University Films, Audio-Visual Center, Indiana University, Bloomington, Indiana 47401.

Sightlines
 Bi-monthly, $8.00. Educational Film Library Association, 17 W. 60th Street, New York, New York 10023. Sent to all EFLA members.

Chapter 17

PROFESSIONAL ORGANIZATIONS

1. American Educational Research Association, 1126 Sixteenth Street, N.W., Washington, D.C.
    Divisions of this organization of behavioral scientists and educators interested in development, application and improvement of educational research are: Administration, Curriculum and Objectives, Instruction and Learning, Measurement and Research Methodology, Counseling and Human Development, History and Historiography, Social Context of Education, and School Evaluation and Program Development.
    Publications: 1) Educational Researcher; 2) Review of Educational Research; 3) American Educational Research Journal; 4) Handbook of Research on Teaching.

2. American Library Association, 50 E. Huron Street, Chicago, Ill.
    Membership open to persons interested in extending and improving library service and librarianship in the United States and throughout the world. The understanding and use of newer media are promoted by the Audio-Visual Committee and the 14 divisions of ALA through research and study, publications, institutes and projects.
    Publications: American Libraries, the official journal of ALA; The Booklist, Choice and Choice Reviews on Cards, Library Technology Reports. In addition many of the divisions publish journals, including: College and Research Libraries, Library Resources and Technical Services, School Media Quarterly, Top of the News, the Journal of Library Automation, and JOLA Technical Communications.

3. Association for Educational Communications and Technology, 1201 Sixteenth Street, N.W., Washington, D.C.
    The AECT is trying to improve instruction through effective use of educational technology. Teacher educators, audiovisual and instructional materials specialists, educational technologists, instructional development specialists,

Professional Organizations 131

audiovisual and television production personnel make up the membership. AECT divisions are segments of the membership organized to represent major educational communications and technology professional interest areas.
Publications: Audiovisual Instruction; the quarterly journal, AV Communication Review; a monthly newsletter, ECT.

4. Association of Chief State School Audio-Visual Officers (ACSSAVO), State Department of Instruction, 1333 W. Camelback Rd., Phoenix, Ariz.
Members are representatives of state departments of education who are in charge of programs and activities associated with the use of audiovisual media in schools in the state.

5. Association for Educational Systems (AEDS), 1201 Sixteenth Street, N.W., Washington, D.C.
Members are interested in systems development. Publication is AEDS Monitor.

6. Association for Supervision and Curriculum Development (ASCD), 1201 Sixteenth Street, N.W., Washington, D.C.
Professional organization of supervisors, curriculum coordinators, directors of curriculum, consultants, professors of education, classroom teachers, principals and others interested in school improvement at all levels of education. A department of the National Education Association.
Publications include: 1) Educational Leadership, 2) Yearbook, 3) News Exchanges, as well as several books through the year.

7. Educational Film Library Association (EFLA), 17 W. Sixtieth Street, New York, N.Y.
Membership includes schools, colleges, public libraries, church groups, labor organizations, film producers, distributors and individuals. Founded in 1943, EFLA serves as the national clearinghouse of information about films, including their production, distribution and use.
Publications: American Film Festival Guide, special monographs and reports, and film bibliographies on selected topics. Access to reference files of EFLA and advisory service.

8. Educational Media Council, Inc. (EMC), 1346 Connecticut Avenue, N.W., Washington, D.C.
The 16 members of the Council are nonprofit national

associations or organizations having a substantial concern with educational media and materials. Serves as a forum for discussion of developments and problems of mutual concern, and as an information clearinghouse. Projects have included publication of the Educational Media Index, an annual Directory of Summer Session Courses on Educational Media, and studies for the U.S. Office of Education on Educational Media in Programs for the Culturally Disadvantaged and Vocational Education.

9. Film Library Information Council (FLIC), 17 W. Sixtieth Street, New York.

Organized in 1967, the Film Library Information Council identifies as its major purposes those of getting the best, the most stirring, the most provocative films in use at the community level, and of working with other organizations to promote greater film use by libraries. Film Library Quarterly is FLIC's official journal.

10. National Association of Educational Broadcasters (NAEB), 1346 Connecticut Avenue, N.W., Washington, D.C.

This association is concerned primarily with radio and television. Today it is more interested in the personal effects of recorded audio and video presentations than in mass effects of media or with broadcasting per se.

Publishes NAEB Newsletter and the bimonthly Educational Broadcasting Review.

11. National Association of Language Laboratory Directors (NALLD), Box E, Brown University, Providence, R.I.

Membership includes anyone whose interests bring him in working contact with the administration or operation of any machine-aided language learning program in an educational institution or governmental agency.

Publication: NALLD Journal. The publications center is a free service to NALLD members.

12. National Society for Programmed Instruction (NSPI). P.O. Box 137, Cardinal Station, Washington, D.C.

The preparation and use of programmed learning materials for schools, industry, the military, government and health sciences are the concerns of members.

Publications include: NSPI Newsletter, NSPI Journal and NSPI Official International Directory of Members.

13. University Film Association (UFA), Audiovisual Center, Dartmouth College, Hanover, N.H.

Membership of the association includes writers, editors, directors, cameramen and technicians producing educational, documentary, scientific and public relations films in colleges and universities. Purposes include promoting an interest in the training and professionalism of film producers in universities, providing a forum for exchange of ideas among this group and with other groups whose interests relate to film production, screening, and evaluating university-produced films, and recording developments and activities in the field.

Official publications include Journal of the University Film Association and a Newsletter of the University Film Association.

Chapter 18

INDEXES

1. Audiovisual Market Place: A Multimedia Guide. R. R. Bowker Co., Annual.
    Hardware manufacturers and software producers and distributors are arranged alphabetically by firm name and in indexes classified by product line. National audiovisual associations and such groups, conventions, and educational radio and television stations are listed. A reference list and a list of serial publications and review services are also included.

2. Books in Print. Volume I: Authors. Volume II: Titles. R. R. Bowker, Annual.

3. Subject Guide to Books in Print. 2 Vols. R. R. Bowker Co., Annual.
    These sources list nearly 400,000 in-print titles by author, title and series. They give publisher and price of book and sometimes the date of publication. These standard tools are very helpful in verifying bibliographic data for practically all U.S. books in print in the English language.

4. Education Index. H. W. Wilson, 1932 to date.
    The Education Index is primarily a periodical index, although it also includes proceedings, yearbooks, bulletins, monographs and many of the United States Office of Education publications. More than 250 educational journals are indexed under such subject areas as: administration, grade level from pre-school to adult education, teacher education, counseling and guidance, curriculum, and subject fields. This index is published monthly except June and August, and the issues cumulate at intervals. Indexed by subject, title and author.

5. Educational Media Council. Educational Media Index. 14 vols. McGraw-Hill Book Co.

Indexes

The Educational Media Index furnishes information on the source, content and cost of non-book materials including programed material, maps, charts, models, etc. The 14 volumes each deal with a specific area: pre-school and primary; intermediate grades; art and music; business education; English language; foreign language; guidance; psychology and teacher education; health, safety and home economics; industry and agriculture; mathematics; science and engineering; geography and history; economics and political science. There is a master title index in volume 14.

6. Educator's Purchasing Master. Vol. I, General: Equipment, Supplies, Services. Fisher Publishing Co., Annual.

Identifies general equipment, materials and supplies used in schools. It lists the availability of these products, the names of their manufacturers, and how the products are marketed. There are four major indexes in this volume: the product index, the manufacturer index, the trade name index and the dealer index.

7. Educator's Purchasing Master. Vol. II, Audio-Visual. Fisher Publishing Co., Annual.

The catalog gives the availability of instructional media and audio-visual equipment, the names of the producers/manufacturers and how the products are marketed.

8. Educator's Purchasing Master. Vol. III, Publishers. Fisher Publishing Co., Annual.

Available instructional materials in specific categories, names of publishers, market information. There is a product index and the publisher index.

9. Index to 8mm. Motion Cartridges. National Information Center for Educational Media, R. R. Bowker Co.

This index lists some 10,000 cartridges, illustrating the importance of this medium to present-day educational curricula. All fully cataloged, including Library of Congress catalog card number.

10. Index to 16mm. Educational Films. National Information Center for Educational Media, R. R. Bowker Co.

11. Index to 35mm. Educational Filmstrips. National Information Center for Educational Media, R. R. Bowker Co.

12. Index to Overhead Transparencies. National Information Center for Educational Media, R. R. Bowker Co.

13. Learning Directory, 1970-71. 7 volumes. Westinghouse Learning Corp.

14. John A. Moldstad, Sources of Information on Educational Media. U. S. Government Printing Office, Superintendent of Documents, Washington, D. C., 1963, as document OE-34024.

15. Multi-Media Reviews Index Supplement, Pierian Press.
    An annual volume published by the Pierian Press, the present volume continuing the updating service begun in the October, 1971 issue of Audiovisual Instruction and supplements coverage contained in the 1971 volume. The publication covers some 70 periodicals and services. Citations contain review ratings.

16. 1970-72 National Center for Audio Tapes with National Center for Audio Tapes 1971 Catalog Supplement. (Formerly National Audio Tape Catalog) University of Colorado.

Chapter 19

ADDRESSES OF PUBLISHERS

Academic Press, Inc.
111 5th Avenue
New York, N.Y. 10003

Acropolis Books, Ltd.
2400 17 St., N.W.
Washington, D.C. 20009

Addison-Wesley Publishing
  Co., Inc.
Reading, Mass. 01867

Aldine Publishing Company
529 S. Wabash Avenue
Chicago, Ill. 60605

American Association for
  Higher Education
Department of Audiovisual
  Instruction
Washington, D.C.

American Association of Colleges for Teacher Education
1201 16 St., N.W.
Washington, D.C. 20036

American Book Company
55 5th Avenue
New York, N.Y. 10003

American Film Institute
John F. Kennedy Center for
  the Performing Arts
Washington, D.C. 20566

American Institutes for Research
Palo Alto, Calif.

American Library Association
50 E. Huron St.
Chicago, Ill. 60611

American University Press
  Service, Inc.
1 Park Avenue
New York, N.Y. 10016

Americana Corp.
Grolier, Inc.
575 Lexington Avenue
New York, N.Y. 10022

Appleton-Century-Crofts
440 Park Avenue S.
New York, N.Y. 10016

Area of Instructional Technology
Syracuse University
123 College Place
Syracuse, N.Y.

Association for Educational
  Communications and Technology
1201 Sixteenth Street, N.W.
Washington, D.C. 20036

Association for Supervision
and Curriculum Development
Department of Audiovisual
Instruction
1201 Sixteenth Street, N.W.
Washington, D.C. 20036

Association Press
291 Broadway
New York, N.Y. 10036

Audio-Visual Associates
Film Review Index
P.O. Box 324
Monterey Park, Calif. 91754

Bantam Books, Inc.
666 Fifth Avenue
New York, N.Y. 10019

Beacon Press
25 Beacon Street
Boston, Mass. 02108

Belknap Press
Harvard University Press
Cambridge, Mass.

Robert Bentley, Inc.
872 Massachusetts Avenue
Cambridge, Mass. 02139

R. R. Bowker Company
1180 Avenue of the Americas
New York, N.Y. 10036

Broadcasting Publications,
Inc.
1735 DeSales Street, N.W.
Washington, D.C. 20036

Bro-Dart Publishing Co.
P.O. Box 923
Williamsport, Pa. 17701

W. C. Brown Company
135 S. Locust Street
Dubuque, Iowa 52001

Burgess Publishing Co.
426 South 6th Street
Minneapolis, Minn.

Business Press, Inc.
32 Broadway
New York, N.Y. 10004

California Association of
Secondary School Administrators
1550 Rollins Road
Burlingame, Calif. 94010

Center for Advanced Study
of Educational Administration
University of Oregon
Eugene, Oregon

Center for Applied Research
in Education, Inc.
70 Fifth Avenue
New York, N.Y. 10011

Center for Architectural Research
School of Architecture
Rensselaer Polytechnic Institute
Troy, N.Y.

Chandler Publishing Company
Division of Intext Education
Publications
College Division
124 Spear Street
San Francisco, Calif. 94105

Chilton Book Company
401 Walnut Street
Philadelphia, Pa. 19106

Addresses of Publishers

Citation Press
50 W. 44th
New York, N.Y. 10036

Columbia University Press
562 W. 113th Street
New York, N.Y. 10025

Computer Instruction
 NETWORK
Salem, Oregon

Council of Europe
Strassburg, Austria

Croft Educational Services
100 Garfield Avenue
New London, Conn. 06320

Crowell, Collier and Macmillan, Inc.
866 Third Avenue
New York, N.Y. 10022

Davis Publications, Inc.
229 Park Avenue S
New York, N.Y. 10003

DCE Publications
Waldo Hall
Oregon State University
Corvallis, Oregon

Dell Publishing Company, Inc.
750 Third Avenue
New York, N.Y. 10017

Doubleday & Company
277 Park Avenue
New York, N.Y. 10017

Eastman Kodak Company
Rochester, N.Y.

EDRS, ERIC Document Reproduction Service
4926 Fairmont Avenue
Bethesda, Maryland 20014

Educational Facilities Laboratories
447 Madison Avenue
New York, N.Y. 10022

Educational Film Library Association, Inc.
17 W. 60th Street
New York, N.Y. 10023

Educational Media Council
1346 Connecticut Avenue, N.W.
Washington, D.C. 20036

Educational Screen, Inc.
434 S. Wabash
Chicago, Ill. 60605

Educational Technology Publications, Inc.
140 Sylvan Avenue
Englewood Cliffs, N.J. 07632

Educator's Progress Service
P.O. Box 497
Randolph, Wis. 53956

Encyclopaedia Britannica, Inc.
425 N. Michigan Avenue
Chicago, Ill. 60611

Entelek, Inc.
42 Pleasant Street
Newburyport, Mass.

ERIC Clearinghouse on Educational Media and Technology
Stanford University
Stanford, Calif.

Fearon Publishers
Industrial Division of Lear
  Siegler, Inc.
6 Davis Drive
Belmont, Calif. 94002

Film Education Resources
  Corp.
1825 Willow Road
Northfield, Ill. 60093

Film Library Information
  Council
P.O. Box 348
Radio City Station
New York, N.Y. 10019

Fisher Publishing Company
Denver, Colorado

The Fund for the Advancement of Education
New York, N.Y.

Gryphon House
Division of Maya Enterprises, Inc.
1333 Connecticut Avenue, N.W.
Washington, D.C. 20036

Halsted Press
Division of John Wiley &
  Sons, Inc.
605 3rd Avenue
New York, N.Y. 10016

Harcourt Brace Jovanovich,
  Inc.
757 3d Avenue
New York, N.Y.

Harper & Row, Publishers
49 E. 33rd Street
New York, N.Y. 10016

Hastings House Publishers,
  Inc.
10 E. 40th Street
New York, N.Y. 10016

Hayden Book Company, Inc.
116 W. 14 Street
New York, N.Y. 10011

William Heinemann Ltd.
400 East 72nd Street
New York, N.Y. 10021

Holt, Rinehart and Winston,
  Inc.
383 Madison Avenue
New York, N.Y. 10017

Houghton Mifflin Company
(Riverside Press, Cambridge)
2 Park Street
Boston, Mass. 02107

Houston University Press
Houston, Texas

Indiana University Press
10th & Morton Streets
Bloomington, Ind. 47401

Information Center on Instructional Technology
Academy for Educational
  Development
1424 Sixteenth Street, N.W.
Washington, D.C. 20036

Institute for Communication
  Research
Stanford, Calif.

Instructional Media Laboratory of America, Inc.
175 Fifth Avenue
New York, N.Y. 10010

Addresses of Publishers

Interstate Publishers
Danville, Ill.

Iowa State Department of Public Instruction
Iowa State University Press
Press Building
Ames, Iowa 50010

Charles A. Jones, Company
Worthington, Ohio

Kendall-Hunt Publishing Company
Dubuque, Iowa

Learning Services
State College, Pa.

Libraries Unlimited, Inc.
Littleton, Colo.

Linnet Books
Hamden, Conn.

Longmans, Green & Company
New York, N.Y.

McGraw-Hill Book Company, Inc.
330 W. 42nd Street
New York, N.Y. 10036

David McKay Company, Inc., Publishers
750 3d Avenue
New York, N.Y. 10017

Massachusetts Institute of Technology
Cambridge, Mass.

Mentor Press
150 Fifth Avenue
New York, N.Y. 10001

C. E. Merrill Publishing Co.
Division of Bell & Howell Company
1300 Alum Creek Drive
Columbus, Ohio 43216

Methuen, Ltd.
London, England

Michigan State University Press
East Lansing, Michigan

Mountain Plains Educational Media Council
University of Colorado
Bureau of Audiovisual Instruction
Stadium Building
Boulder, Colorado 80302

MSS Educational Publishing Company
19 E. 48th Street
New York, N.Y. 10017

National Art Education Association
1201 16 Street, N.W.
Washington, D.C. 20036

National Association of Independent Schools
4 Liberty Square
Boston, Mass. 02109

National Center for Film Study
1307 S. Wabash Avenue
Chicago, Ill. 60605

National Observer
Dow-Jones Books
Box 300
Princeton, N.J. 08540

National School Public Relations Association
1201 Sixteenth Street, N.W.
Washington, D.C. 20036

National Security Industrial Association
740 Fifteenth Street, N.W.
Washington, D.C. 20005

New York State Education Department
Division of Educational Communications
Albany, N.Y.

Northwest Library Service, Inc.
Eugene, Oregon

Northwestern University Press
1735 Benson Avenue
Evanston, Ill. 60201

Ohio Department of Education
518 South Wall Street
Columbus, Ohio 43215

Ohio State University
156 W. 19th Avenue
Columbus, Ohio 43210

Oregon State System of Higher Education
Oregon State University Press
Box 689
101 Waldo Hall
Corvallis, Ore. 97330

Outerbridge and Dienstfrey
200 W. 72nd Street
New York, N.Y. 10023

Oxford University Press, Inc.
200 Madison Avenue
New York, N.Y. 10016

Parker Publishing Company
Sub. of Prentice-Hall, Inc.
West Nyack, N.Y. 10994

F. E. Peacock Publishers
Itasca, Ill.

Pergamon Press, Inc.
Maxwell House, Fairfield Park
Elmsford, N.Y. 10523

George A. Pflaum, Publisher
38 W. Fifth Street
Dayton, Ohio 45402

Phi Delta Kappa
Eighth and Union
Bloomington, Indiana

Philosophical Library
15 E. 40th Street
New York, N.Y. 10016

Pierian Press
Box 1808
Ann Arbor, Mich. 48106

Pitman Publishing Corporation
6 E. 43rd
New York, N.Y. 10017

Prentice-Hall, Inc.
Route 9W
Englewood Cliffs, N.J. 07632

Producers Guild of America
141 El Camino Drive
Beverly Hills, Calif. 90212

Addresses of Publishers 143

Purdue University
Educational Psychology Section
South Courts, G
Lafayette, Indiana 47907

Rand McNally & Company
Box 7600
Chicago, Ill. 60680

W. B. Saunders Co.
218 W. Washington Square
Philadelphia, Pa. 19105

Scarecrow Press, Inc.
52 Liberty Street
Metuchen, N. J. 08840

Schocken Books, Inc.
67 Park Avenue
New York, N. Y. 10016

W. W. Schwann
137 Newbury Street
Boston, Mass. 02116

Charles Scribner's Sons
597 Fifth Avenue
New York, N. Y. 10017

Silver Burdett Company
250 James Street
Morristown, N. J. 07960

Simon & Schuster, Inc.
630 Fifth Avenue
New York, N. Y. 10020

Something Else Press, Inc.
Elm Street
Millerton, N. Y. 12546

Southeastern Educational Corp.
3450 International Blvd.
Atlanta, Ga.

Special Devices Center
Port Washington, L. I.
New York, N. Y.

Stanford University
Stanford, Calif. 94305

Superintendent of Documents
Government Printing Office
Washington, D. C. 20402

Syracuse University Press
Box 8
University Station
Syracuse, N. Y. 13210

Systems Development Corporation
Santa Monica, Calif.

Tab Books
Blue Summit, Pa.

Teachers College Press
Columbia University
New York, N. Y.

Teaching Research
Monmouth, Oregon

Charles C. Thomas
301 E. Lawrence Avenue
Springfield, Ill. 62703

Time, Inc.
Time-Life Building
Rockefeller Center
New York, N. Y. 10020

TMI Institute
Albuquerque, New Mexico

United States Atomic Energy Commission
Washington, D. C. 20545

U. S. Department of Health,
Education and Welfare
Office of Education
Washington, D. C. 20036

University of Birmingham
National Center for Programmed Learning
School of Education
Birmingham, England

University of Chicago Press
5801 Ellis Avenue
Chicago, Ill. 60637

University of Colorado
Boulder, Colorado

University of Connecticut
Storrs, Conn. 06268

University of Illinois
Urbana, Ill. 61801

University of Maryland
Press
College Park, Maryland

University of Michigan
Press
615 E. University Avenue
Ann Arbor, Mich. 48160

University of Missouri
Press
Columbia, Mo.

University of Nebraska
Press
Lincoln, Nebraska 60508

University of Oregon, Books
Eugene, Oregon 94703

University of Rochester
School of Liberal and Applied Studies
Rochester, N. Y. 14627

University of Texas Press
Visual Instruction Bureau
Austin, Texas

University of Wisconsin-
Milwaukee Press
Milwaukee, Wisc.

Van Nostrand-Reinhold Company
450 W. 33d Street
New York, N. Y. 10001

Ward Lock Educational
London, England

Westinghouse Learning Corp.
Department D
100 Park Avenue
New York, N. Y. 10017

WGBH Educational Foundation
Boston, Mass.

John Wiley and Sons, Inc.
605 3d Avenue
New York, N. Y. 10016

H. W. Wilson Company
950 University Avenue
New York, N. Y. 10003

INDEX OF AUTHORS

Allen, Dwight W. 112
Allison, Mary L. 12
American Association of School Librarians 174
American Film Institutes 52
Anderson, Robert M. 13
Antan, Eleanor M. 243
Arrasjid, Harun 184
Association for Supervision and Curriculum Development, 1965 Yearbook Committee 175
Association for Supervision and Curriculum Development, Seventh Curriculum Research Institute 238
Atkinson, R. C. 106
Axeen, Marina E. 185

Bailey, Catherine M. 176
Baker, Eva L. 221, 222, 223
Baker, Robert L. 198
Banathy, Bela H. 199
Barnes, O. D. 107
Barnouw, Erik 1
Barson, John 200
Beck, Lester F. 53
Beilby, Albert 15
Bennik, F. D. 132
Berthold, Jeanne Saylor 239
Bitzer, D. L. 108
Bjerstedt, Ake 88

Bloodworth, Mickey 186
Bloom, Benjamin S. 201, 230, 257, 276
Bower, G. H. 249
Briggs, Leslie J. 109, 202, 240, 258
Brown, G. W. 110
Brown, James W. 17, 155, 177, 187, 287
Brown, Louis H. 178
Bruner, Jerome 241, 242
Bryan, G. L. 111
Bushnell, Don D. 112, 203

Calder, Clarence R. 243
Caldwell, Joseph H. 156
Calvin, Allen C. 89
Campbell, Donald T. 259
Campeau, R. L. 109, 202, 240, 258
Carlson, Richard O. 2
Carnegie Commission on Higher Education 188
Carpenter, C. R. 260, 261
Carter, C. M. 113
Center for Architectural Research 220
Charnes, A. 18
Chisholm, Margaret E. 19
Christiansen, Lina J. 156
Clark, Richard E. 114
Cochran, Lee W. 160
Cook, Desmond L. 204
Cook, Myra B. 156
Costello, Donald P. 54

Costello, Lawrence F. 55
Coulson, John 115, 116
Culbertson, J. A. 262
Cullum, Albert 157
Curran, Mary Alice 239

Dale, Edgar 158, 244
Danielson, Wayne A. 263
Davies, Ivor K. 189
deCecco, John P. 90, 264
deKieffer, Robert E. 159, 160
De Korte, D. A. 56
Department of Audio-Visual Instruction 57
Diamond, Robert M. 58
Dreyfus, Les S. 265
Dunn, W. R. 91
Dwyer, Francis M. 190

Edling, Jack V. 205, 206, 207, 266
Educational Media Council 59
Edwards, Allen L. 267
Ely, Donald P. 191, 211
Engel, Gerald W. 117
Erickson, Carlton W. H. 23, 24, 262, 279
Eurich, Alvin C. 288

Feingold, Samuel L. 132
Feldhusen, John H. 118
Ferkiss, Victor C. 289
Fiore, Quentin 295
Firth, Brian 162
Flores, Ivan 119
Footlick, Jerrold K. 290
Frederiksen, Norman 231
Freedman, Florence B. 26
Fry, Edward B. 92
Frye, Charles H. 132
Fund for the Advancement of Education 93

Gage, Gerald 208
Gagné, Robert M. 109, 202, 209, 210, 240, 245, 246, 258, 268, 269
Garner, Wayne Lee 94
Gattegno, Caleb 247
Gaver, Mary V. 27
Gerard, R. W. 120
Gerlach, Vernon S. 191, 211
Giannetti, Louis D. 60
Gilliom, Bonnie Cherp 61
Giraud, Chester 62
Glaser, Robert 95, 212, 270
Godfrey, Eleanor P. 3
Good, C. V. 271
Goodlad, John I. 121
Gordon, George N. 55
Gottesman, Ronald 63
Great Plains National Instructional Television Library 28
Grobman, Hulda 232
Gronlund, Norman E. 213
Gruenberger, Fred 122
Guss, Carolyn 35, 36

Haga, Enoch 214
Hanna, Paul R. 163
Harcleroad, Fred F. 155
Harrison, J. A. 272, 291
Hastings, J. T. 230
Heneley, S. P. 262
Herbert, John David 164
Hickey, Albert E. 123
Hicks, Bruce L. 124
Hieronymous, Ramelle 135
Hilgard, Ernest R. 248, 249, 250, 273
Hoban, Charles F., Jr. 274
Hoffer, Jay 64
Holtzman, Wayne H. 125
Holznagel, Donald 126
Homine, Lloyd E. 165
Hood, Stuart 65
Huss, Roy 66

Index of Authors

Institute for Communication Research 275
Institute for Development of Educational Activities 127
Iowa State Department of Public Instruction 180

Jacobs, Paul I. 96
Jarvis, Oscar T. 166
Jones, J. C. 251
Jones, Milbrey L. 29
Jordan, Robert T. 292
Joyce, Bruce R. 167
Judy, Stephen 68

Kaufman, Roger A. 233
Kemp, Jerrold E. 215
Kent, Graeme 168
Kinder, James S. 169
Knirk, Frederick G. 234
Knowlton, James Q. 216
Komoski, Kenneth 97
Krathwohl, David R. 276

Lamb, Robert Thomas Bryden 4
Lange, Phil C. 98, 277
Lanier, Vincent 30
Lekan, Helen 128
Lessinger, Leon 235
Lewis, Richard B. 155
Lewis, William C. 69
Lieberman, Irving 192
Liebert, Robert M. 70
Lifton, Walter M. 293
Lindquist, E. F. 278
Loughary, John W. 218, 294
Lysought, Jerome P. 99

McBeath, Ronald J. 6
McBride, Wilma 71

McClintock, Susan 138
McClosky, Mildred G. 193
McGowan, William N. 181
MacLean, Roderick 72
MacLennan, Donald W. 79, 281
McLuhan, Marshall 195, 196, 197
Madaus, G. F. 230
Mager, Robert F. 219, 279
Maier, Milton H. 96
Markle, D. G. 129
Martin, W. T. 5
Masia, Bertram B. 276
May, Mark A. 109, 202, 240, 258
Maynard, Richard R. 73
Meetham, Roger 298
Milkman, Robert L. 280
Miller, Richard I. 299
Millerson, Gerald 74
Mills, Belen C. 170
Mills, Ralph A. 170
Moir, Guthrie 75
Molnar, Andrew 130
Morgan, Robert 131
Mountain Plains Educational Media Council 31
Mueller, Theodore H. 100
Murray, H. T., Jr. 303
Murray, Thomas 171

National Association for Educational Broadcasters 76
National School Public Relations Association 300
Niemi, John A. 301
Norberg, Kenneth D. 177
Novak, J. 303

Oringel, Robert S. 77

Pasich, Timothy 135
Paulson, Casper F. 236

Pipe, Peter 101
Platt, John R. 302
Plunkett, Dalton 33
Popham, W. James 221, 222, 223
Postlethwait, S. N. 78, 303
Pula, Fred John 7

Reid, J. Christopher 79, 281
Rogers, Miriam 135
Rosenbaum, J. 132
Rossi, Peter H. 304
Rossoff, Martin 305
Rostow, Eugene V. 306
Roucek, Joseph S. 102
Routt, Edd 80
Rowell, John 34
Rufsvold, Margaret I. 35, 36

Saettler, Paul 8
Salomon, G. 282
Saravevic, Tefko 225
Schueler, Herbert 194
Schuller, Charles Francis 42
Sherman, Beverly 130
Shutz, Richard E. 198
Siegel, S. 283
Sippes, Patrick 133
Smith, Karl U. 307
Stanley, Julian C. 261
Stolorow, Lawrence 96, 134
Stufflebeam, Daniel L. 237
Sullivan, Peggy 182
Swarthout, Sherwin G. 171

Taber, Julian I. 103
Tansey, P. J. 226
Taylor, Calvin W. 252
Thornton, James W. 81, 187, 195, 287, 308

Tobias, Sigmund 284
Tobin, M. J. 104
Torrey, George N. 172
Travers, Robert M. W. 253, 254
Trow, William Clark 9, 285
Trump, J. Lloyd 10
Tyler, I. Keith 309

United States Atomic Energy Commission 39
University of Colorado 37, 38
Unwin, Derick 11
Uttal, William 135

Van Hoffman, Nicholas 196, 310
van Ormer, Edward B. 274
Visonhaler, John 136
Voight, Ralph C. 227

Wade, Serene E. 82
Wagner, Richard V. 83
Wagner, Robert W. 286
Weisgerber, R. A. 228, 229, 255, 256
Westinghouse Learning Corporation 40, 217
WGBH Educational Foundation 84
White, David 85
Wigren, Harold E. 86
Wilkenson, Cecil E. 183
Williams, Catherine M. 309
Wilson, H. A. 106
Winan, Raymond V. 41
Wittich, Walter Arno 42, 173
Woolman, Lorraine 87
Wyman, Raymond 184

Zinn, Karl L. 137, 138

INDEX OF TITLES

Accountability: Policies and Procedures, Learner Centered Management Support Systems 235
Administering Educational Media 177
Administering Instructional Media Programs 23, 161, 179
Adoption of Educational Innovations 2
The Affective Domain, A Resource Book for the Media Specialist 197
Aids to Modern Teaching: A Short Survey 4
The American Film Institute's Guide to College Courses, 1969-1970 52
Aspects of Educational Technology 11, 91
Association for Educational Communications and Technology 105
The Audio-Tutorial Approach to Learning 78, 303
Audiovisual Instruction 159
Audiovisual Materials: Their Nature and Their Use 173
Audio-Visual Methods in Teaching 158, 244
Audiovisual Resources for Teaching 15
Audiovisual Resources for Teaching Instructional Technology: An Annotated Listing 14
Automated Educational Systems 214
The Automation of School Information Systems 203
AV Instruction: Media and Methods 17, 155

A Basic Reference Shelf on Instructional Media Research 266
A Basic Reference Shelf on Learning Theory 248
The Best of ERIC: Recent Trends in Computer-Assisted Instruction 114
Blackboard to Computer: A Guide to Educational Aids 168
Blue Book of Audiovisual Materials 16
The Business of Radio Broadcasting 80

The Celluloid Curriculum: How to Use Movies in the Classroom 73
The Celluloid Weapon: Social Comment in the American

Film 85
The Classroom Teacher's Guide to Audio-Visual Materials 26
Closing the Gap--Research and Practice 265
Combined Film Catalog, 1972 39
Come-Alive Classroom: Practical Projects for Elementary Teachers 156
Computer Assistance for Instruction: A Review of Systems and Projects 137
Computer-Assisted Instruction: A Book of Readings 106
Computer-Assisted Instruction: Annotated Bibliography 107
Computer-Assisted Instruction: A Selected Bibliography and KWIC Index 117
Computer-Assisted Instruction: A Survey of the Literature 123
Computer-Assisted Instruction, Testing and Guidance 125
Computer-Assisted Instructional Management 116
Computer Based Instruction 134
Computer-Based Instruction in Statistical Inference, Final Report 132
Computer Education Resource Catalog 126
Computer in American Education 112
Computer Software: Programming Systems for Digital Computers 119
Computerized Bibliography of Mass Media 263
Computers and Communications--Toward a Computer Utility 122
Computers and Education 111
Computers and Education: A Workshop Conference at University of California, Irvine 120
Computers and Information Systems in Education 121
A Conceptual Scheme for the Audiovisual Field 216
The Conditions of Learning 209, 245, 269
Costs of Installing and Operating Instructional Television and Computer-Assisted Instruction in Public Schools 113
Curriculum Improvement and Innovation: A Partnership of Students, School Teachers and Research Scholars 5
Cybernetic Principles of Learning and Educational Design 307

Demonstration of the Use of Self-Instruction 165
Designing Instructional Strategies for Young Children 170
Development of the Bell System First-Aid-and-Personal Safety Course 129
Developmental Efforts in Individualized Learning 228
Dimensions of Teachers' Attitudes toward Instructional Media 284

Index of Titles

Early Window: Effects of TV on Children and Youth 70
Educating for Tomorrow: The Role of Media, Career Development and Society 293
Education--A New Era 290
Educational Aspects of Simulation 226
Educational Communication in A Revolutionary Age 309
Educational Communications Handbook 176
Educational Evaluation and Decision Making 237
Educational Measurement 278
Educational Media and You 183
Educational Media for the Preschool Child 53
Educational Media Index 20
Educational Media Selection Centers: Identification and Analysis of Current Practices 34
Educational Research: New Perspectives 262
Educational System Planning 233
Educational Technology 88, 264
Educational Technology and the Teaching-Learning Process 239
Educational Technology: Readings in Programmed Instruction 90
Educational Television, The Next Ten Years 275
Educator's Guide to Free Guidance Materials 20
Educator's Guide to Free Tapes, Scripts and Transcripts 20
Edunet: Report of the Summer Study on Information Networks Conducted by the Interuniversity Communications Council 110
The Effect of Different Television Utilization Procedures on Student Learning 82
The Effect of Video-Taped Single Concept Demonstrations in an In-Service Program for Improving Instruction 87
Elementary School Library Collection 27
Entelek CAI/CMI/PI Information Exchange 22
Entering Audiovisual Competencies 280
Essentials of Learning 253
Establishing Instructional Goals 221
European Research in Audio-Visual Aids, Part I, Bibliography 291
European Research in Audio-Visual Aids, Part II, Abstracts 272
Evaluation Activities of Curriculum Projects: A Starting Point 232
Experimental and Quasi-Experimental Designs for Research 259
Extending Education Through Technology: Selected Writings by James D. Finn on Instructional Technology 6

Film Catalog, 1973-1975 31
The Film Experience 66
Films and Filmstrips on Audio-Visual Materials and Methods 25
Focus on Change: Guide to Better Schools 10
For Radio and Television Broadcasting 77
Four Case Studies in Programmed Instruction 93
The Fourth Revolution: Instructional Technology in High Education 188
Fundamentals of Teaching with Audiovisual Technology 24

Generative Computer-Assisted Instruction 135
Geography in the Teaching of Social Studies 163
Guide for Improving Visualized Education 190
Guide to Evaluating Self-Instructional Programs 96
Guide to Free Filmstrips 20
Guide to Instructional Television 58
Guide to Programmed Instruction
Guide to the Literature on Interactive Use of Computers for Instruction 138
Guidebook to Film 63
Guidelines for Audio Tape Libraries 38
Guides to Educational Media 36
Guides to Newer Educational Media: Films, Filmstrips, Kinescopte, Phonodiscs, Phonotapes, Programmed Instruction Materials, Slides, Transparencies, Videotapes 35

Handbook of Research on Teaching 268
Handbook on Formative and Summative Evaluation of Student Learning 230
Highlights of Schools Using Educational Media 186
High School 1980: The Shape of the Future in American Secondary Education 288
History of Broadcasting in the United States 1
History of Instructional Technology 8

The IMC--Whose Empire? 184
Improvement of Teaching by Television 76
Index for Bibliography of Computer Applications in Education 136
Index to Computer Assisted Instruction 128
Individualized Instruction: A Manual for Administrators 205
Individualized Instruction Case Studies 206
Individualized Instruction Slide-Audio Tape Sets 207
Information Retrieval: The Essential Technology 298
Inquiry: Implications for Televised Instruction 71

Index of Titles

Instructional Design, A Plan for Unit and Course Development 215
Instructional Film Research, 1918-1950 274
Instructional Film Research Reports 260, 261
Instructional Materials 41
Instructional Media and Creativity 252
Instructional Media: A Procedure for the Design of Multi-Media Instruction, A Critical Review of Research and Suggestions for Future Research 109, 202, 240, 258
Instructional Media: Theory-Application 172
Instructional Process and Media Innovation 255
Instructional Product Development 198
Instructional Resources for Teachers of the Culturally Disadvantaged and Exceptional 13
Instructional Systems 199
Instructional Systems Development 200
Instructional Technology: A Book of Readings 234
Instructional Technology: Its Nature and Use 42
Integrated Teaching Materials 171
Introduction to Educational Research 271
Introduction to Information Science 225
Invitation to Learning 227
ITFS: What It Is ... How to Plan 67
ITV Humanities Project: A History of Five Experimental Programs for Instructional Television 84
ITV: Promise Into Practice 61

Learning 251
Learning about Learning 241
Learning and Individual Differences 246
Learning and Programmed Instruction 103
Learning Directory 217
LP II--A Goal Programming Model for Media 18

Man-Machine Systems in Education 218, 294
Man, Media and Machines: The Teacher and His Staff 167
Management of Learning 189
Man's Information System 254
Manual of Audio-Visual Techniques 160
Mass Media and Adult Education 301
Mass Media in the Classroom 162
Media Indexes and Review Sources 19
Media Objectives for Teachers 184
Medium Is the Massage 295
Memo on Film 54
Model for Establishing a Priority of Educational Needs 208
Multi-Media Reviews Index 32

Multiuniversity: A Personal Report on What Happens to Today's Students at American Universities 196, 310

New Directions for School Administration 181
New Educational Materials, Pre-Kindergarten Through Grade 12 12
New Media and College Teaching 81, 195, 208
New Media and Education 304
New Media and Higher Education 187, 287
New Relationships in Instructional Television 59
New Spaces for Learning 220
1972 Recorded Instruction for Television 28
1972-1973 Learning Directory Supplement 40
Nonparametric Statistics for the Behavioral Sciences 283
Nurturing Individual Potential 238

On Using Computers to Individualize Instruction 133
Organization and Operation of Broadcast Stations 64

Perception and Change: Projections for Survival 302
Perspectives in Individualized Learning 229, 256, 299
Plan for Progress in the Media Center 180
Planning an Instructional Sequence 222
A Position Paper on CAI Research and Development 118
Practical Programming 101
Preparing Objectives for Programmed Instruction 219, 279
President's Task Force on Communications Policy, Final Report 306
Problems and Methods in Programmed Learning 104
Problems in School Media Management 182
Proceedings of Project ARISTOTLE Symposium 127
Proceedings of the Seminar on Programmed Learning 100
Proficiency Tests for Training Evaluation in Training Research and Education 231
Program Evaluation and Review Technique Applications in Education 204
Programmed Instruction 94, 277
Programmed Instruction: Bold New Venture 89
Programmed Instruction: 1967 Yearbook of the National Society for the Study of Education, Part II 98
Programmed Instructional Materials for 1964-1965: A Guide to Programmed Instructional Materials Available for Use in Elementary and Secondary Schools as of April, 1965 97
Programmed Learning and Computer-Based Instruction: Proceedings of the Conference on Applications of Digital Computers to Automated Instruction 115

Programmed Teaching: A Symposium on Automation in Education 102
Psychological Principles in Systems Development 210
Psychomotor Domain, A Resource Book for the Media Specialist 224
Push Back the Desks 157

Research in Instructional Television and Film 79, 281
Review of Educational Applications of the Computer, Including Those in Instruction, Administration and Guidance 131
Role of Supervisor and Curriculum Director in a Climate of Change 175

School Library and Educational Change 305
Series of Motion Picture Documents of Communication Theory and the New Educational Media 286
Some Pedagogical and Engineering Design Aspects of Computer-Based Education 108
Sources of Audiovisual Materials 29
Standards for School Media Programs 174
State of Educational Technology: 1961-1966 3
Stating Behavioral Objectives for Classroom Instruction 213
Stimulus Ideas for Using Selected Educational Media 33
Strategy for Evaluation Design 236
Study of Systemic Resistance to Utilization of ITV in Public School System 83
Study of the Production and Use of Video-Taped Materials in the Training of In-Service and Pre-Service Teachers of English 68
Study to Determine the Feasibility of Developing a Coordinated Distribution System for Audio-Tape Recorded Materials 178
A Survey of Instructional Closed-Circuit Television 57
Survey of Television 65
System for Analyzing Lessons 164
Systematic Instruction 223

Taxonomy of Educational Objectives 257
Taxonomy of Educational Objectives, Handbook I: Cognitive Domain 201
Taxonomy of Educational Objectives, Handbook II: Affective Domain 276
Teach with Television: A Guide to Instructional TV 55
Teacher and the Computer 124
Teacher and Technology: New Design for Learning 9, 285
Teacher Education and New Media 194

Teaching and Media: A Systematic Approach 191, 211
Teaching and Television: ETV Explained
Teaching Library Use to Undergraduates--Comparison of
  Computer-Based Instruction and the Conventional Lecture
  185
Teaching Machines and Programmed Instruction 92
Teaching Machines and Programed Learning, I and II: Data
  and Directions 95
Teaching Machines and Programmed Learning, II 212
Teaching Strategies and Classroom Realities 193
Techniques and Activities to Stimulate Verbal Learning 243
Techniques of Attitude Scale Construction 267
Technique of Lighting for Television and Motion Pictures 74
Technological Man 289
Technology in Education: Challenge and Change 7
Technology in Education: Education U.S.A. Special Report
  300
Television and Radio 62
Television in Education 72
Television in Education and Training 56
Theories of Learning 249, 273
Theories of Learning and Instruction 250
Through Cable to Classroom: A Guide to ITV Distribution
  Systems 69
Tomorrow's Library: Direct Access and Delivery 292
Toward a Theory of Instruction 242
Toward a Visual Culture: Educating Through Television 247
Training Research and Education 270
Transitional Elementary School and Its Curriculum 166

Understanding Media: The Extension of Man 296
Understanding Movies 60
Use of Newer Media in Art Education Project 30
Using Audio-Visual Materials in Education 169
Using Instructional TV: Elementary, Kindergarten and Nursery Education 86

Verbi-Voco-Visual Explorations 297

What Does It Do To Johnny? 282
A Working Bibliography of Commercially Available Audio-
  Visual Materials for the Teaching of Library Science 192